TSC

P9-DBS-909

Little Kids—Powerful Problem Solvers

Little Kids—Powerful Problem Solvers

Math Stories from a Kindergarten Classroom

Angela Giglio Andrews
Paul R. Trafton

HEINEMANN
Portsmouth, NH

Heinemann

361 Hanover Street
Portsmouth, NH 03801–3912
www.heinemann.com

Offices and agents throughout the world

© 2002 by Angela Giglio Andrews and Paul R. Trafton

All rights reserved. No part of this book may be reproduced in any form or by any electronic or mechanical means, including information storage and retrieval systems, without permission in writing from the publisher, except by a reviewer, who may quote brief passages in a review.

The authors and publisher wish to thank those who have generously given permission to reprint borrowed material:

Excerpts from *Principles and Standards for School Mathematics* published by the National Council of Teachers of Mathematics (2000) are used with permission of the publisher.

Library of Congress Cataloging-in-Publication Data
Andrews, Angela Giglio, 1945–
    Little kids—powerful problem solvers : math stories from a kindergarten classroom / Angela Giglio Andrews, Paul R. Trafton.
       p. cm.
    Includes bibliographical references.
    ISBN 0-325-00431-5 (acid-free paper)
    1. Mathematics—Study and teaching (Preschool). 2. Problem solving.
I. Trafton, Paul R. II. Title.

QA135.6 .A53 2002
372.7'2—dc21

2001039919

Editor: Victoria Merecki
Production: Elizabeth Valway
Cover design: Greenleaf Illustration & Design
Typesetter: Kim Arney Mulcahy
Interior and cover photos by Angela Giglio Andrews
Manufacturing: Steve Bernier

Printed in the United States of America on acid-free paper

13   12   11   10   09   VP   11   12   13   14   15

We dedicate this book to our youngest grandchildren,
Sarah Marie and Kaitlyn Marie Andrews,
Zoe Marie and Anna Catherine Frantom,
and Jillian Marie Trafton—our favorite
little kids and powerful problem solvers!

Contents

Foreword / xi

Acknowledgments / xv

About the Book / xvii

1 **Little Kids—Powerful Problem Solvers** 3

  Mathematical Capabilities of Young Children / 3

  Characteristics of Classrooms / 4

  Kindergartens as Mathematical Learning Sites / 6

  The Role of Play in Developing Mathematical Competence / 8

  Summary / 8

2 **September—Which Holds More?** 11

  Setting the Stage / 11

  The Lesson / 12

  Looking Back . . . / 15

  About the Mathematics / 16

3 **October—The Dilemma of Sharing Cookies** 19

  Setting the Stage / 19

  The Lesson / 20

  Looking Back . . . / 24

  About the Mathematics / 24

4 **November—It's Not Fair!**
They've Got More Blocks .27

  Setting the Stage / 27

  The Lesson / 28

Looking Back . . . / 31

About the Mathematics / 32

5 December—When Is a "Triangle" a Triangle? 37

Setting the Stage / 37

The Lesson / 38

Looking Back . . . / 42

About the Mathematics / 43

6 January—Soup with Chicken Inside 47

Setting the Stage / 47

The Lesson / 47

Looking Back . . . / 51

About the Mathematics / 52

7 February—The Secret of the Hearts 55

Setting the Stage / 55

The Story / 56

Looking Back . . . / 60

About the Mathematics / 61

8 March—Ms. McGill's Challenge 63

Setting the Stage / 63

The Lesson / 64

Looking Back . . . / 68

About the Mathematics / 69

9 April—Aaron and the Tall Tower 73

Setting the Stage / 73

The Investigation / 74

Looking Back . . . / 78

About the Mathematics / 79

10 May—"Dear Bus Barn" 83

Setting the Stage / 83

The Problem / 83

Looking Back . . . / 90

About the Mathematics / 91

11 June—Revisiting the Rice Table 93

Setting the Stage / 93

The Lesson / 93

Looking Back . . . / 100

About the Mathematics / 101

References / 103

Foreword

At a time when teachers are being subjected to unrelenting pressure to prepare their pupils for standardized achievement tests, Angela Andrews and Paul Trafton show us vividly how to respond to it without resorting to mind-deadening worksheets and dreary arithmetic drills. We are given detailed examples of how accountability for a set of formal national standards in mathematics can be approached with real respect for kindergarten children's needs and capabilities.

Together Andrews and Trafton address the daily intricacies of launching kindergartners on a life of what they call mathematical "sense making." In the process they show us how their strategies address the standards in the NCTM's *Principles and Standards for School Mathematics* introduced to the nation in 2000.

The book presents ten stories, one for each month of the school year. Each story recounts how children in Andrews' kindergarten class tackled a particular mathematical problem. As I began reading the book I did not anticipate that by the time I reached the story in the December chapter, when the kindergartners struggle with the question "When is a triangle a triangle?", I would want to join a cheering section to encourage their efforts—so easily are readers brought into the unfolding interactions and events in the classroom. By December we become familiar with many of the children, and we appreciate many of their individual differences as well as the way their teacher struggles with her own role in their labors.

Several major themes are threaded throughout the stories. One theme is the importance of believing in children's natural capacities and in-born dispositions and to make sense of their experiences. The way Andrews and Trafton provide a mathematically rich environment and classroom climate and challenge the children to solve the mathematical problems around them are excellent illustrations of the important distinction between academic and intellectual goals and activities in the curriculum. Far too often, policy decision makers and curriculum designers fail to grasp this major distinction: academic goals address small bits of information and facts that, though eventually useful and important, tend to discourage if not blunt young children's intellectual dispositions. The intellectual dispositions in action in this classroom include making sense of experience and observations, estimating, predicting, hypothesizing, analyzing, and applying a variety of mathematical concepts richly illustrated for us in this book; their development requires opportunities to be engaged in solving problems that have meaning in that the children are addressing practical problems in ways that are clearly purposeful to them. In the day-to-day life of this class, their teacher's deep belief in the children's mathematical capabilities is actually and repeatedly put to the test in practical and visible ways.

The authors' term "hard fun" captures their appreciation for the way the children approach the problems they take on. By way of example, one of the problems arising toward the end of the school year is how the children accept responsibility for figuring out how many seats will be needed and how many are available on the bus that will take them on their field trip to the zoo. Because their school district regulates the number of adults to children when field trips are taken, they are propelled into the issues of ratio and processes of calculations and finding good ways to represent their results. In this way the children master basic academic skills related to numeracy in the service of achieving intellectual goals that clearly interest them.

Another important theme throughout the stories is the real meaning of the concept of a community of learners. Curriculum developers and other educators so often advocate making the classroom into a community of learners that it has almost become a cliché. But Andrews and Trafton bring this concept to life fully as we are informed of how children assist as well as challenge each other. More often than not, in these stories, children are helping each other master some basic mathematical concepts as they argue, help and occasionally hinder each other, and strive to solve the practical problems on their agenda. The rich quality of the classroom life and the role of the children's interactions with one another are made very clear in each story. The authors help us see so well the power of classroom discourse that allows the knowledge and understanding of one child to become accessible to the others.

Another theme is the clear evidence the stories provide of young children's willingness to persevere and persist until the problems they deal with have been addressed to their satisfaction. The experiences of Andrews and Trafton as documented throughout this book clearly suggest that adults, including teachers of young children, often underestimate children's capacities to gain deep satisfaction from hard work. Indeed, the children themselves refer to their experiences in this wonderful classroom as "hard fun." As readers we share their reverses, setbacks, and triumphs and become enlightened by it all and come to appreciate their capacities for persistence in the face of challenge.

Perhaps the themes already mentioned would not be possible were it not for another important one, namely Andrews' long-established habit of reflecting on her own decisions, dilemmas, and choices. Each story ends with reflections on the mathematics involved in the story, showing clearly the importance of the authors' conviction that unless teachers understand the mathematics involved in the problems the children are tackling, they will not be able to support them adequately and to capitalize on the opportunities at hand. As Andrews and Trafton point out, if teachers listen respectfully to the children and then honestly question them about their thinking, children will learn to defend it. In addition, Andrews shares her frequent dilemmas concerning whether to help one group and let another struggle without her presence, or to join a new group and possibly lose the "teachable moment" emerging in the group she'd be leaving behind. Surely all teachers of young children recognize her anguish over this and the many other dilemmas faced by the teacher of young children. How should the teacher's time be divided among the children and the small working groups? In addition, Andrews shares with readers the occasions when it is very tempting to tell a child an answer to a question rather than let her take up the struggle to solve it. She describes other moments when she asks herself whether or not to interfere with the strategy a group of children have adopted as a way to solve a problem. Invariably we are given the opportunity to enjoy the fruits of her wise choices in these difficult situations.

As Andrews and Trafton point out, mathematics allows us to generalize beyond the seen to the unseen. These stories and the reflections upon them that the authors share provide rich sources of generalizing from the experiences of one kindergarten class to all other classes to which young children bring their sense-making dispositions.

Lilian G. Katz, Ph.D.
Professor Emerita,
Co-Director, ERIC/EECE
University of Illinois

Reference

National Council of Teachers of Mathematics (NCTM). 2000. *Principles and Standards for School Mathematics.* Reston, VA: NCTM.

Acknowledgments

First, we want to thank the kindergarten children of Scott School, whose enthusiasm for mathematics and wonderful mathematical insights have been an inspiration for Angela over several years and led her to write this book. We also want to express appreciation to the faculty and administration of the school for their support—in particular, Angela's teammates, Helen Hocking and Terry Musial, who participated regularly in discussions about their teaching and the work of children.

There were three individuals who made direct contributions to the book and to whom the authors are indebted: Robin Frisch and Abby Hub, whose technological skills were indispensable, and Mary Friedrich, who transcribed audiotapes and helped prepare the manuscript for submission. We express deep appreciation for their efforts.

Last, but certainly not least, we are deeply grateful to our spouses: Bill Andrews encouraged Angela to pursue her dream of creating a book that would inform other educators, and Patricia Trafton encouraged Paul's interest in collaborating with Angela. Moving from ideas to a book is a slow process with many bends and dips in the road. Knowing that we had their ongoing support and encouragement throughout the process was vital in creating, shaping, and writing this book.

About the Book

This book celebrates the mathematical capabilities and achievements of kindergarten children through 10 stories that describe their learning, problem solving, and reasoning. The stories provide examples of what school mathematics can be for young children and what they can do when they have a mathematically rich classroom environment.

The overall goals of the book are to increase the awareness of early childhood educators, educational leaders, and parents to the possibilities of what *can* be with respect to learning mathematics and to the mathematics that children can do. We hope to

- Engage, by drawing readers into the mathematical events described in the book.
- Inform, through greater awareness of what young children can do and the nature of instruction that promotes their learning.
- Promote reflection, about what is occurring, the work of the children, and about creating classrooms that present developmentally appropriate and challenging mathematical experiences.
- Inspire, as we become excited about the potential of young children and their work.

The opening chapter discusses the capabilities of children and characteristics of classrooms that promote the work described in the stories. This is followed by the stories. The stories occurred over several years, although some stories involve the same group of children. One story is presented for each month of the school year to indicate to teachers when it occurred with respect to the school year.

Each story consists of 4 parts. The first section, "Setting the Stage," provides the background or context for each story—what led to the experience and observations by the teacher about the children or the motivation for a lesson. This is followed by the investigation or event, which is told in narrative form including classroom discourse and teacher observations. The story or lesson is followed by a "Looking Back . . ." section in which Angela Andrews shares some of her thoughts about the lesson and discusses some of her decisions. The final section, "About the Mathematics," written by Paul Trafton, highlights the mathematics that was involved and the mathematical reasoning of the children. An awareness of the mathematics and how children think about it is important. This knowledge enables teachers to highlight important ideas, plan additional experiences, assess children's insights, and build on their patterns and strategies with all of the children.

Selected quotes from *Principles and Standards for School Mathematics* (NCTM 2000)[*] have been used throughout the book to highlight important ideas about the teaching and learning of mathematics. Both authors have been closely associated with the NCTM standards, Paul as chair of the K–4 writing team for the 1989 document and Angela as a member of the pre-K–2 writing team for the 2000 document.

The stories in this book represent a wide variety of mathematical experiences. Many of them are set in real-world and physical contexts. Some are structured lessons while others occur in daily classroom situations. The experiences should not be viewed as model lessons that can be replicated in another classroom or show ideal teaching. The lessons are real, complete with bumps, unexpected events, and complex decisions. They were selected to highlight the children's thinking and capabilities. In her classroom, Angela also has lessons that address necessary skills and "pull the children's thinking together." Finally, these are "regular" children (*not* gifted kids) representing several socioeconomic backgrounds and ethnic origins. Some of them, like Aaron (chapter 9), are mathematically advanced, while others, like Rebecca (chapter 7), have to work hard. They're just children who really like mathematics, like to solve challenging math problems, and believe that thinking is "cool."

---

[*] *Quotations from* Principles and Standards for School Mathematics *(NCTM 2000) are used with the permission of the publisher.*

Most students enter school confident in their own abilities, and they are curious and eager to learn more about numbers and mathematical objects. They make sense of the world by reasoning and problem solving, and teachers must recognize that young students can think in sophisticated ways. Young students are active, resourceful individuals who can construct, modify, and integrate ideas by interacting with the physical world and with peers and adults. They make connections that clarify and extend their knowledge, thus adding new meaning to past experiences. They learn by talking about what they are thinking and doing and by collaborating and sharing their ideas.

—Principles and Standards
for School Mathematics (75–76)

1

Little Kids—Powerful Problem Solvers

Mathematical Capabilities of Young Children

Young children are capable mathematical thinkers and problem solvers. They are inventive, thoughtful, and curious risk takers as well. They particularly love to solve problems that engage and challenge them and will work on challenging tasks for extended periods of time. Papert (1996) captures young children's love of challenging work in the following interchange between a kindergarten child who was leaving the computer lab following an initial computer experience and a child who was waiting with his class to enter the room.

> [The child waiting to enter the room asked,] "What was it like?" The friend replied, "It was fun." Then paused and added: "It was really hard." The relation between "fun" and "hard" may need some interpretation. Did this mean "it was fun in spite of being hard" or "it was fun because it was hard"? The teacher who heard the tone of the conversation and knew the children had no doubt. The child meant it was "fun" because it was "hard." It was "hard" and this made it all the more "fun." Since then I have listened to children with an ear sensitized by this experience and have come to know that the concept of *hard fun* is widely present in children's thinking. (53)

This perspective on young children's mathematics capabilities is in sharp contrast to the traditional perception that teachers should "keep it simple," so as not to confuse or upset them. Unfortunately, this viewpoint has often dominated our perception of young children, limiting the mathematics we allow them to explore and the kind of problems they solve in school. The work of kindergarten children in the 10 stories that constitute this book will surprise many readers, for they don't fit the traditional view. The initial response may well be surprise followed by disbelief. Some may think, "This can't be," or "These must be gifted children." However, this is not the case. These are typical children doing what seems natural to them.

The shift in our view of young children from fragile learners to robust thinkers changes the way we work with them and the experiences they have. In this chapter, we explore the characteristics of classrooms that support and promote mathematical reasoning. We also discuss the unique opportunities kindergarten teachers have to establish classrooms that truly meet children's mathematical needs.

Characteristics of Classrooms

What is there about Angela Andrews' classroom that causes children to engage in in-depth discussions about mathematics, solve complex problems, and deal informally with concepts that are not typically introduced until several years later? In this book, you'll find kindergarten children solving problems involving division and remainders (chapter 3), holding an in-depth discussion about whether a pizza slice is a triangle (chapter 5), discovering number patterns (chapter 9), and using thoughtful strategies to compute (chapters 8 and 9). Here we will briefly examine some of the characteristics of classrooms devoted to helping children make sense of mathematics.

The notion that mathematics can be learned with understanding— that is, that learners can make sense of mathematics—is a surprise to many adults. Yet, when children make sense of mathematics, they develop deep understanding of important ideas. This means making connections with their informal mathematical knowledge and making connections among mathematical ideas. Thus, they not only surprise us by learning mathematics beyond our perceptions of what kindergarten children can learn, they also learn it better. They develop great confidence in themselves as capable problem solvers and thinkers. They come to expect mathematics learning to be a sense-making experience and therefore they are willing to spend a great amount of time on challenging problems and tasks.

There are many characteristics of classrooms that help children make sense of mathematics. An appropriate environment is much more than just doing activities or using manipulatives. These are important, but only to the extent that *doing* leads to *thinking* about relationships and concepts. Let's examine some of the characteristics of these classrooms.

Letting children take ownership of tasks and problems—that is, letting them use their own approaches and strategies—is important in helping them to understand. Their ideas almost always make sense to them and thus contribute to their learning. We often struggle when their ways are not the most efficient ones in our eyes. Yet over time, as children have a chance to work with and listen to other children, immature strategies become more mature.

Providing sufficient time to work on tasks is also important. Children often need repeated opportunities to work on, tinker with, and mess about with ideas before they make sense. This time may occur in an extended period during one day or over several days, weeks, or months. In this book, the rice table stories (chapters 2 and 11) show the power of an ongoing approach to measuring capacity. Also, the multiple graphing experiences that occur over 3 days involving Rebecca and Tommy (chapter 7) illustrate this point.

Sense-making classrooms provide many opportunities for children to reflect and communicate. Reflecting (really thinking about what one is doing) and communicating (sharing one's ideas and listening to the ideas of others) are powerful elements in helping *all* children learn successfully. This serious, in-depth thinking and sharing is highlighted in the story about what makes a triangle a triangle in chapter 5. As children prepare to share ideas, they have to clarify the ideas for themselves; and as children hear the thinking of other children, they develop new mathematical insights. By talking about mathematics together, children learn respect for the ideas of others and come to believe that thinking is a "cool" thing to do.

Surrounding children with a rich variety of tools to assist them as they work is also important. These tools include a wide variety of manipulates as well as hundreds charts, calculators, computers, and paper and pencils. These tools need to be available at all times. Further, children should be allowed to select the tools that make sense to them and use them in ways that make sense to them.

In sense-making classrooms the teacher's role changes. Teachers need to be keen observers of children's work, so they can assess the level of learning and make appropriate plans. Teachers also need to judge when to let children work and when to provide information and closure. They need to encourage children through questions and genuine interest in their work. Conducting whole-class seminars in which children share their thinking requires new skills. They also need to make decisions about how to help *all* children make sense out of the thinking of one child, how to encourage *all* children to participate, and how to use sharing time as teaching time. Above all, teachers need to show a deep respect for children's ideas and hold a deep-seated belief that all children can learn mathematics.

The ideas discussed in this section lead to establishing a community of mathematics learners and a climate that promotes learning and supports risk taking. Children thrive in such classrooms, learn mathematics successfully, and become confident and resourceful problem solvers.

Without such an environment, the stories in this book would not have occurred.

Kindergartens as Mathematical Learning Sites

Kindergarten has always held a special place in the hearts of most adults. Even the word *kindergarten* calls forth in children and adults alike feelings of excitement, optimism, and purpose. This first year of formal schooling is the launching pad for great cognitive, social, and emotional adventures. Kindergarten can provide wonderful opportunities for children to make sense of the world and advance their learning. It is a unique place where individuals come together for the first time to form a community of learners. Listen to Angela's unique memories of kindergarten as seen through a window.

> I never went to kindergarten. There wasn't one in the parochial school that my brothers attended, but there was a public school kindergarten near my home that my best friend attended. Each day I would walk up to that school to meet him and then we'd walk home together. I always tried to get there early so I could peek at what was going on inside. I remember pressing my nose to the window and peering in to see that feast for my young eyes. I saw easels, blocks, tricycles, a book nook with lots of pillows, a play kitchen, wooden puzzles, and big, thick crayons. The children were busy and happy and the teacher moved among them comfortably and purposefully. I knew even then that this was a wonderful place—a learning place. Even fifty years later, that remembered image of kindergarten still brings back feelings of warmth and excitement.

Kindergartens can be places where children and mathematics are brought together in unique ways. Teachers need to understand kindergarten children and mathematics and bring these two together in mutually respectful ways. In order to do this, decisions need to be made about *space*, *things*, *time*, and *climate*.

Space and Things

The space and things in a kindergarten classroom are unique in that it is not typically outfitted with desks arranged in neat rows. There is usually some space for moving about the room, an area where the class can comfortably meet together, and materials unique to kindergarten, such as unit blocks and a housekeeping center. Teachers have to be creative in arranging the space so that it is neither chaotic nor unmotivating.

Traffic patterns and the physical placement of centers must be carefully considered in order to provide an environment where children can "bump into mathematics" wherever they go, whether it's at the block corner, the rice table, the book nook, or the puzzle shelf. However, if the mathematics they bump into is to be meaningful, it is not enough to just immerse kindergarten children in an environment filled with materials. Math materials must be carefully selected and planned for. Teachers also should have a sense of whether the math materials will further the children's thinking. The rice table lesson (chapter 2) and the block-building problem (chapter 4) provide evidence of this.

Time

Time is another unique element of kindergarten. Within some constraints, such as half-day kindergarten, the way the time is spent is determined, at least to some extent, by the teacher. In some of the stories, Angela, like most kindergarten teachers, grouses about the pressure of limited time. However, teachers must provide adequate time and opportunities for children to develop, construct, revisit, test, and reflect on their growing mathematical understandings. They also have to recognize that different students need different amounts of time, as the story of Rebecca and Tommy illustrates (chapter 7).

Climate

Finally, kindergarten provides a unique opportunity for teachers to establish a wonderful learning climate for young children who have very few preconceived attitudes about how learning should occur. Children come to kindergarten ready, willing, able, and eager to learn and they depend on their teachers to make that learning happen. The learning climate that teachers establish depends on their own attitudes toward learning and children. These attitudes, conscious or otherwise, are picked up by the children and this, in turn, establishes the climate. If teachers indicate by words and actions that they value thinking, so will the children. If teachers expect that when young children open their mouths they will have something important to say, the children will talk. If teachers respectfully listen to and then honestly question children about their thinking, the children will learn to defend it. If teachers encourage children by their words and tasks to think *deeply* about simple things, the children will learn to be deep thinkers. If teachers model a risk-taking approach to mathematics where errors are expected, respected, and inspected, children will feel free to join in the fun! When teachers establish a climate for learning that encourages cooperation, collaboration, risk taking, questioning, discourse, doing, thinking, and reflecting, children are free to learn in mind-engaging ways that make mathematics meaningful and sensible.

The Role of Play in Developing Mathematical Competence

A historically unique characteristic of kindergarten has been its emphasis on learning through play. Structured learning experiences must be balanced with opportunities for play. Kindergarten children need to assimilate the language, relationships, and ideas that they are confronted with. For this reason, regularly scheduled, self-directed play periods are important.

Sometimes play time is confused with the romantic notion of "hands-off" play, where adults let children "do whatever they want to do." Play time should involve choice—about what children will do, with whom they will do it, and how long they will do it before moving to another activity. However, there are several roles for teachers that ensure the activities of play time are purposeful.

The first role is setting the stage for play. Teachers have to create an environment that provides lots of opportunities for children to construct, explore, investigate, test, and practice. They have to stay alert to their children's ideas and interests and provide materials that lend themselves to developing these ideas and interests further.

A second role is to be available during play. This is not the time to be doing other tasks. Without interfering too much with the natural dynamics of children's play, teachers have to be available to add cognitive elements and intervene appropriately when necessary to keep the play alive and growing. Teachers can extend a concept from a lesson or pose an additional challenge to push children's thinking further. They also have to help children who may be having difficulty making or sustaining relationships in play and occasionally even help a child make choices or maintain active, but self-controlled, participation.

A third role for teachers is carefully observing the play and using these observations to inform their teaching. As children play, they learn to design, organize, understand, compare, evaluate, choose, explain, and communicate. By carefully observing these behaviors, teachers can make plans to extend the concepts children encounter in play situations. They also can gain important information about the children's interests, strengths, and areas of weakness that will help them present ideas to the children in a way that is neither too overwhelming nor insufficiently challenging.

Summary

Throughout the kindergarten year, children are learning more than just mathematics. They learn a lot about the nature of mathematics—what it is, what it means to do it, and their view of themselves as math students.

The attitudes they develop now will strongly influence their future mathematical performance and whether they choose to continue their study of mathematics. If children experience sense-making mathematics here, they will come to think of mathematics as a sense-making experience. If they experience interesting, powerful mathematics here, they will come to view mathematics as the interesting and powerful endeavor that it can be.

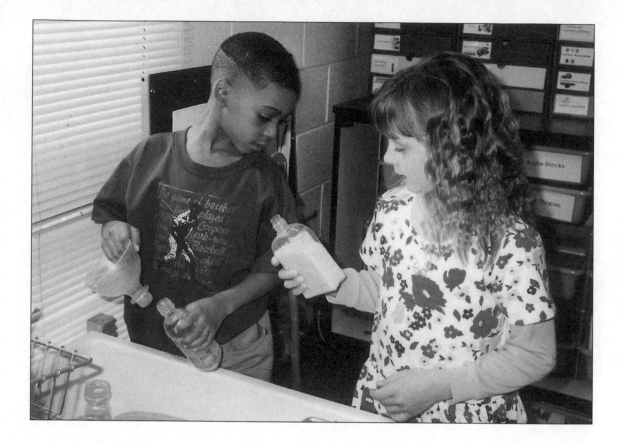

Teaching that builds on students' intuitive understanding and informal measurement experiences helps them understand the attributes to be measured as well as what it means to measure. A foundation in measurement concepts should be established through direct experiences with comparing objects, counting units and making connections between spatial concepts and number.

—*Principles and Standards*
for School Mathematics (103)

2

September—Which Holds More?

Setting the Stage

Children just love to measure. They compare how far they can jump, how tall they are, how many cubes they can hold in their hands, and whether they can pick each other up (despite my admonitions not to do so). These natural experiences are a beginning point for learning more about length, height, capacity, and weight. Because of the importance of measurement I begin the work early in the year and continue to use activities that require measurement throughout the year. Thus, for me, measurement is much more than an isolated unit of work.

This story focuses on the children's introduction to the rice table, where they explore ideas about capacity. However, the children's observations and conjectures make the lesson far more than just an introduction to a measurement activity. The heart of the story lies in the children's struggles to understand the physical phenomena of liquids and solids and how they behave. Important, too, are the teacher's efforts to help the children make sense of the mathematics rooted in the experience and, at the same time, to begin to set the stage for the children's mathematical discourse—listening and speaking with one another about big mathematical ideas.

My rice table is the typical large plastic bin filled with rice, but I have given a great deal of thought about how to set it up and maintain it. I have carefully assembled a collection of clear plastic jars and bottles. Some are tall and thin, like olive jars; others are short with wide mouths, like peanut butter jars. I have some that are cylindrical in shape and some that are shaped like rectangular prisms. Several of them have interesting features, such as larger diameters at the base than at the lip. There are also measuring cups, scoops, funnels, and a small dustpan and broom to clean up rice spills. A sign stating that two children may work here at a time hangs over the table. The center is in a quiet corner of the room, because children do serious work here and don't want to be disturbed.

The Lesson

We began by discussing safety and housekeeping rules. We discussed why the jars and bottles were made of plastic rather than glass and why the children shouldn't use glass jars at home unless they had their parents' permission. We also discussed the importance of keeping the rice inside the bin. Next I demonstrated how to clean up the area, sweeping all the loose rice from the floor into a dustpan and then into the trash can. I also explained that children should empty all jars after working with them so the center will be ready for the next person to use.

The Shapes of Jars and Bottles

To help children make the connection between the shapes of the containers and their function in everyday life, I chose two containers. I held up a tall, thin bottle and asked, "What do you think came in this bottle?"

"Ketchup," said Christian. "We got that kind at home," he whispered to Kirsten, who was sitting beside him in the circle.

"What about this one?" I asked the children, holding up a short jar with a wide mouth.

"Oh, peanut butter comes in that," Brett said confidently.

Next I pointed to the ketchup bottle and asked, "Do you think peanut butter might ever come in this bottle? Talk about that with your neighbor."

After a few moments the children seemed ready to share their thinking. "It would be too hard to get out," Kunal said, summing up the idea I had heard expressed by several children.

"Why do you say that?" I inquired.

"Because peanut butter won't pour," he quickly responded.

"Yeah—you could stick a knife in there and get some, but then you couldn't reach the rest!" Lindsey added.

"You could hit it on the bottom," Sammy suggested.

"But it still wouldn't come out. You'd have to add water and shake it," Lindsey said, with a voice of authority.

"Even ketchup is hard to get out of there!" Sarah added.

"Well, yes, it is sometimes!" I agreed. "I am wondering if we could put ketchup in the peanut butter jar?"

Several children laughed at the idea. Leslie noted "You'd make a big mess!" and another child added "Yeah, it would come out too fast!"

"So you're saying this tall, thin bottle is better for holding wet things like ketchup, but this short, wide jar is better for holding dry things like peanut butter?" My statement introduced a new idea for the children to think about: the relationship between the kind of ingredient and the shape of the container.

Which One Holds More?

Now I wanted to shift the discussion to focus on these two containers in terms of capacity, so I asked, "I wonder which of these containers holds more rice?"

"That's easy," Jeff said, "the tall one!" Most of the other children nodded their heads in agreement. I wasn't surprised by this response because young children tend to equate being taller with holding more, without considering other attributes.

"Sarah, I wonder what you are thinking about this question. Which do you think will hold the most rice?" I directed this question to Sarah, a somewhat shy child who didn't speak often unless called upon. Sarah seemed unsure. Finally she said, "I think maybe not. I think the other one will hold more." By "other one," she meant the peanut butter jar.

Aha, I thought, *Sara has noticed that the peanut butter jar is much wider than the ketchup bottle and realized that height and width must be considered together.* I wanted her to share her thinking with the others. "That sounds like an interesting idea. Tell us more about what you are thinking, Sarah."

"Well . . . ," she responded, "ketchup is wet, but peanut butter is dry. It's like rice. So maybe the peanut butter jar will hold more rice."

Wow, I certainly hadn't expected that response! From my perspective, Sarah's response was illogical, yet several children nodded their heads in agreement. I knew we couldn't resolve this issue today, and I reminded myself that children need many hands-on experiences before focusing on relevant attributes of containers in terms of capacity. Also, I wondered if I had distracted them by concentrating on what each jar contained. Anyway, it was clearly time to focus on how capacity is measured.

About How Much Does Each One Hold?

"Hmmm . . . let's see how much the ketchup bottle holds," I said as I picked it up. I showed the children the small orange coffee scoop that I had planned to use as a unit of measure and demonstrated how to get a level measure by drawing my finger across the top.

"My mom always does that too!" Nabihah said excitedly.

Unable to resist seeing where this would go, I asked, "Why do you suppose she does that?"

"Maybe so it won't spill off the top," Kunal suggested.

"To make it come out right?" Kristen asked.

"So it will be even," Nabihah answered confidently. Kindergarten children understand *even* to mean *fair*, so the others accepted this idea without question.

I poured the scoop of rice into the ketchup bottle, demonstrating how to use a funnel to guide the rice through the bottle's narrow neck. After adding one scoop, I held the bottle up and drew the children's attention to the level of the rice. I asked the children to use this information to estimate how many scoops of rice they thought would fill the bottle.

This was the first time I had used the word *estimate*, so I explained what it meant. "When you estimate you use what you know to figure out *about* how many. You don't have to know exactly how many, but you do have to think of something that makes sense. Do you think it would make sense if I said this bottle would hold 100 scoops?"

"That would be way too much!" several children said.

"What about 0 scoops?" Everyone seemed to understand that was not sensible.

"You can see there is already 1 scoop inside and there's a lot more room," Cameron explained.

This seemed like a good time to introduce the difference between estimating and guessing. "If you had a blindfold on and couldn't see the bottle or the scoop, you would have to guess how many scoops would fill the bottle. But you have eyes to see with and a brain to think with, so you can estimate!"

Several children offered estimates at this point; most of them were reasonable. I called individual children (the fidgety ones) to join me in adding more scoops to the bottle. As the bottle filled, the children watched the level of the rice carefully and some of them adjusted their estimates accordingly. As the last scoop filled and overflowed the bottle, I took the opportunity to introduce another important idea about measurement: that it is approximate.

"Oh," I exclaimed, "this bottle holds *almost* 8 scoops," modeling language that indicates approximation.

> Understanding that all measurements are approximations is a difficult, but important concept for students.
>
> *Principles and Standards for School Mathematics* (46)

Putting aside the ketchup bottle, I focused the children's attention on the peanut butter jar. "And NOW!," I announced dramatically, "ABOUT how much do you estimate this jar will hold? Remember, an estimate doesn't have to be exact. It just has to make sense. Take a minute to think about it and then whisper your estimate to your neighbor."

The children seemed eager to think about this, and most seemed to have an estimate, although it was clear that they didn't all agree. We repeated the process of filling the jar with rice, with different children coming up to add a level scoop to it.

"It's going be more! I know it!" Sarah said, watching the rice level slowly rise.

My first thought was, *What do I do about this? She is going to be right for the wrong reason!*

"I think it's gonna be 10," Lindsey said as the eighth scoop went in.

After the jar was filled and it was discovered that, indeed, it did hold more than the bottle, many of the children seemed amazed. Sarah was sure that her reasoning about the jar was confirmed, for I heard her say to a friend, "If we used water, the ketchup bottle would hold more!"

Rather than correct her, I had her present her new idea to the class. From the looks on the children's faces and their comments, I could tell that some agreed, some strongly disagreed, and others were unsure. Since time was running out, I decided to turn the question back to the children. "Sarah has given us something interesting to think about. While you are working at the rice table this year, I would like for you to think about what she said and see if you agree or disagree."

> Teachers should guide students' experiences by making the resources available, planning opportunities to measure, and encouraging students to explain the results of their actions.
> *Principles and Standards for School Mathematics* (103)

While I knew that many children would spend their time, at least initially, simply filling and emptying containers, some would count the scoops as they filled the containers and perhaps make comparisons between containers. I suspected that a few would experiment with Sarah's idea and try to prove or disprove it. I also knew that we would revisit her idea in the days and weeks ahead.

Looking Back . . .

I took my entire math time to introduce this center, but I knew that the time invested in establishing the group rules would pay off throughout the year. I also had been able to present some important measurement concepts and engage the children in interesting—and surprising—thinking about the capacity of containers. In addition, I had learned a lot about the thinking of my children.

Estimation was one of the big ideas that I wanted to introduce. I wanted the children to understand that there is no such thing as a right or wrong estimate. When the children began to use additional evidence to adjust their prior estimates, I was very pleased. It showed me they were using estimation as a vehicle for thinking, not guessing.

Sarah's unexpected comment forced me to make a quick decision: Do I correct her or move on? It's hard for me to resist the natural tendency of adults to correct children's misconceptions on the spot, but I felt that correcting her at that moment wouldn't solve anything. First, I don't think it would have changed her mind. Second, if I wanted my children to take risks, I couldn't be telling them they are wrong when they express their ideas. Turning the idea back to the children seemed more productive. It would give them some serious food for thought as they worked at the rice table and would help me assess their thinking as they worked.

As usual, reflecting on this experience informed my instruction. I had always used rice because it is easier and less messy than using water. Now I could see that I needed to add water to the table occasionally so that the children could test their thinking about wet and dry ingredients' effects on capacity. This experience also confirmed my belief that measuring experiences must be made available throughout the year. It would take time for the children to work on the big ideas that had been introduced today.

Finally, I didn't expect, but was pleased by, the seriousness of the children's conversation. They were willing to share, listen, and wrestle with big ideas. This was going to be a great year!

About the Mathematics

The children's experiences described in this lesson illustrate several important aspects of the mathematics of measurement. Teaching measurement begins by helping children understand the measurable aspects of an object. A ketchup bottle, for example, has several measurable attributes: how tall it is (height), how heavy it is (weight), and how much it holds (capacity). Children have to understand what is meant by each of these attributes. This lesson begins with a discussion of what is meant by capacity then moves to an informal discussion of which container held more. (In the case of length, for example, a pencil and a ruler would be lined up at one end and then one would find which object extended farther.) Later, children will use direct comparison by filling one jar and pouring its contents into a second jar to see which holds more. This lesson illustrates that capacity is not an intuitively obvious idea and developing an understanding of it does not occur quickly.

The lesson then focuses on the measurement process. It is easy to determine the number of cubes a person is holding in her hand by counting, for cubes are discrete and easily countable. However, attaching a number to a continuous attribute is more complex. First, we must agree on what to call 1 and that is an arbitrary decision. In this lesson "1 orange scoop" was chosen to be the unit of measure. The use of a different-size scoop would result in a new measurement.

Measuring involves finding how many units are contained in the object, as this lesson showed. In the case of length, it might mean finding how many paper clip units fit along the object. For capacity, it might mean how many orange scoops a container "holds." This process allows us to describe the "how muchness" of a bottle or jar using a number and a unit, for example, *8 scoops.* The process of measuring any attribute is essentially the same and children at all levels need to understand it. The power of measurement is that it allows us to attach numbers to continuous attributes and use numbers to make comparisons. Expressing capacity as a measurement (a *number* of *units*) is a more advanced level of comparing the capacity of two containers. For example, bottle A holds 8 scoops and jar B holds 10 scoops, so jar B is "bigger" with respect to capacity.

Two other fundamental ideas are also introduced. One is the idea that all measurement is approximate, and this is not a simple idea. Filling containers is a good way to initially illustrate that measurement is not exact. Emphasizing this idea in multiple contexts over many years enables children to grow in their understanding of its meaning.

Estimation is the second idea. It involves using a benchmark, such as the amount that 1 scoop or 3 scoops fill to make an inference about the total number of units. Thus, it is much more than a wild guess. When children estimate, they use intuitive ideas of fractions and ratios. For example, if 3 scoops fill a little less than half the container, they reason that double that amount would *about fill* the container, and thus estimate the capacity to be 6 or 7 scoops.

This informal, exploratory experience with capacity was enjoyable for both the children and the teacher. However, the lesson also involved important mathematics. Understanding the mathematics enables teachers to emphasize key ideas and important language. Children often have trouble with measurement throughout school and just try to memorize names of units and relationships among them. One way of changing this situation is to ensure that the proper foundation is established at the very beginning. Thus, kindergarten instruction needs to provide ongoing focus on and substantial time for the process of measurement.

Problem solving is natural to young children because the world is new to them, and they exhibit curiosity, intelligence, and flexibility as they face new situations. The challenge at this level is to build on children's innate problem-solving inclinations and to preserve and encourage a disposition that values problem solving.

—Principles and Standards
for School Mathematics (116)

3

October—The Dilemma of Sharing Cookies

Setting the Stage

I loved the book *The Doorbell Rang*, by Pat Hutchins (1986), the first time I read it—both for its story and for the delightful, purposeful illustrations with their many patterns. I was sure my children could relate to this story of two children faced with the dilemma of sharing cookies between themselves and with other children who come to visit. I put the book in my "Be sure to read with the class" pile.

One day, when the children were in PE class, a mother dropped by the room with a surprise treat for her daughter's birthday: 2 boxes of Teddy Grahams™ cookies. I decided that this would be perfect time to read *The Doorbell Rang*. After reading the book, I would have the children share these cookies. But how would they go about this? I didn't have much time left before the children returned to the classroom—definitely not enough time to count out the cookies. Also, I noticed as I took the boxes out of the bag that there were two different kinds: vanilla and chocolate. This would complicate things! Then I made a decision, partly due to limited time and partly to provide a new level of challenge for my children, to put a handful of each kind into containers for each group and let the children take it from there, remainders and all. I would be taking a risk. There would probably be leftovers in some of the containers, and the children would have to create their own ways of dealing with this problem. Of course, it also meant trusting them not to eat the cookies until they had been shared fairly. Would the children be able to deal with the mathematics involved in such a problem? Well, I was about to find out!

As it was still early in the year, my plan also would allow me to learn more about how well my five groups of children worked together. I could observe who the leaders were and whether the groups had a good balance in terms of capabilities and the ability to work together. The lesson would also provide the opportunity for them to cooperate and come to consensus about carrying out the task. As I put out the cookies, I began to formulate plans in my mind for introducing the task to the children.

The Lesson
Introducing the Story

I heard the children returning so I quickly grabbed the book and sat in my rocking chair. I was excited to see how this lesson would turn out. The sight of a new book plus the gleam in my eyes must have made the children curious and eager; they didn't make the usual requests for drinks of water, but quickly sat down by my chair instead. The story begins with Ma offering a tray of cookies to Victoria and Sam to share. The number of cookies is not shown in the illustration, nor is it mentioned in the text, but on page 2 of the book, Sam and Victoria state, "That's six each."

"There's 12 cookies!" Brett blurted, "She gave them 12 cookies."

I was surprised at the speed at which Brett had determined the number of cookies, and from the nods of several other children, I could tell that they had figured this out too. I hadn't expected the children to become engaged in the mathematics of equal shares on the first read through. I had planned to pause during my rereading of the story in order to help the children do this. Obviously, they had other plans.

I continued the story. The doorbell rang again and Ma opened it to find two more children standing there. Before I could even read the next line, Claire chimed in, "Now they have to share again. They'll only have 3 each."

"How did she do that so quickly?" I thought. I looked up to see Claire and several other children using their fingers. Claire had put up 3 fingers on each hand. Another child had put up all 5 fingers on his left hand. Then he held up another finger on his right hand and put that finger across the two fingers from the left hand. "3," he agreed.

As I continued the story, reading the part where 2 more children came to the door, the children seated on the floor around me continued their calculations. I noticed that the children were using several methods to find the number of cookies that 6 children would get. Several children had paired up, each contributing 6 fingers to stand for cookies. Other children were laying their spread-out fingers on the floor as they thought about the problem. I noticed one child touching 6 of his fingers to his chin twice as he counted to 12. Of course, I also noticed that some children were just happy to wait until the text revealed how many cookies each child would share. I returned to the story, reading the part where 2 more children arrived with 4 cousins. The children groaned! "Oh no!" Delon said. "Tell Ma to stop answering the door. They're only gonna get one now!" I couldn't resist asking why he thought so.

"Well, they only got two last time, so they have to get one now," he replied.

"Na-ah! They could get between one and two. I get that sometimes," Elizabeth countered.

"I think there's 12 kids now. There was 6," said Jeff, holding up 6 outstretched fingers. "Then 2 more came." Two more fingers popped up. "Then they brought 4 cousins. That's 2 more and . . ." He ran out of fingers at this point.

"And 2 more makes 12!" Kelly chimed in.

"Yeah," Jeff agreed.

I was surprised at how quickly many of the children were able to solve the problems presented in the story. As we progressed through the book, going from 2 children to 4 children to 6 children to 12 children, I never had to ask how many cookies my students thought each child would get. They saw the cookie sharing as an interesting problem to solve and they didn't need my coaxing to dive in!

Sharing Cookies

At this point I held up a plate of cookies and explained where the cookies came from. Then I posed my problem to the children. "I will give each table a plate of cookies. You must first think of some fair ways to share the cookies and maybe try out some of your ideas. When the people at your table agree that you have shared the cookies fairly, raise your hands and I will come and listen to your sharing plan. If, after explaining your method to me, you still agree that it is a fair way to share the cookies, then I will give you permission to eat them. Please do not eat any cookies, or even any crumbs, until you have told me about your plan."

> The decisions that teachers make about problem-solving opportunities influence the depth and breadth of students' mathematics learning.
>
> —*Principles and Standards for School Mathematics* (119)

I picked up my observation clipboard and began to circulate. Some of the things I wanted to observe included the following:

Did each child participate?

Which children tended to be leaders and which tended to be followers?

Which children thought of strategies that were creative or showed a strong understanding of mathematics concepts?

Did the children at each table seem to work well together?

As the children were washing their hands and settling in to work on the problem, I wondered what would happen and what approaches they would take. As I moved from table to table, I was interested in listening to their thought processes. At one table I heard four different plans. One child suggested, "We can deal them like cards until they run out." I don't think he had considered that the cookies might not come out even. When trying out this idea, I heard them counting, "1, 1, 1, 1, 1, 2, 2, 2, 2, 2, 3, 3, . . ."

Another child offered, "We can all take some and see if the piles look even." In the minds of other children in his group, this was not considered fair, as a child with a bigger hand would take more. A third child suggested estimating. We had done a lot of work with estimating and the children were beginning to understand that an estimate is not an exact amount, but "you try a number and see." To them this meant choosing a reasonable number, such as five cookies each, and checking to see if they needed to take more. A fourth plan, a variation of the "dealing out" and estimating approaches, was to give a small number of cookies, such as 2 or 3, to each child and continuing from that point, dealing them out one at a time.

In September we had done a lot of work with patterns, so I wasn't surprised when one group tried out a plan involving patterns. The notion of patterns seemed to be tied to the fact that there were two kinds of cookies. I didn't quite understand what Josh meant by "We'll pattern," but it worked perfectly. Josh gave each child a white one (vanilla) and then a brown one (chocolate), and so on. Instead of stating the total number of cookies each would receive, they reported it as 3 vanilla and 4 chocolate. When they lined the cookies up, the lines sometimes weren't the same length, but the fact that each line had 3 vanilla and 4 chocolate cookies convinced them that the number was the same.

As I jotted down these observations, I noted that in the process of devising and implementing various plans, the notion of fairness was of great importance to my students. They certainly understood the principle of fair shares! This principle led to one of the most fascinating of all strategies.

"That's not fair! You're taking all chocolates!" Jeff accused.

This outburst drew me over to Jeff's group to see what the issue was. This group had decided to pass the tub around, with each child taking one cookie each time. Well, Jeff had noticed that Natalie was taking only chocolate cookies.

"I like chocolate!" said Natalie, defending her choices.

"So do I!" Jeff said. "But you can't take all chocolates!"

"Well, it's my favorite," countered Natalie, seemingly unable to understand what the fuss was all about. This led to an "exchange" of viewpoint about fairness that went beyond the mathematical notion of equal shares.

After much discussion, her group agreed that Natalie's approach was not fair to the group. They decided that if she were going to take only chocolate cookies, she couldn't take as many cookies. So they devised a point system in which a chocolate was worth 2 points and a vanilla was worth 1 point. The group decided to try assigning each person 5 points, but Natalie realized that this plan wouldn't work. "I can't use all my points for chocolates with 5!" she complained. So the group tried 6 points, and Natalie got to take 3 chocolate cookies. Can you imagine how hard it was for the children to explain this approach to one another? But they got it—they all got it! I was amazed given the complexity of the strategy. Thank goodness the cookies came out even at that table.

Dealing with Leftovers

Coming out even wasn't the case for the other tables. It was fascinating to see the various ways that children dealt with leftover cookies (i.e., remainders). Breaking cookies in half was one approach. One group of five children had 3 cookies left over. They broke these cookies in half (as close to half as they could get) and gave each person an extra half. They concluded that was close enough and decided to give the extra half cookie to the one who dealt them out.

In one group, five children had 6 cookies and the sixth child, Elizabeth, had 5 cookies. "I'll give her one of mine," Jenny said, helpfully.

The other children followed suit. Now they faced a new—and surprising—problem. "Hey! Now you have too much!" Delon said.

Indeed, Elizabeth now had 10 cookies and the five other children had 5 cookies each. It didn't take long for the group to decide that this was absolutely *not* fair, and back to the drawing board they went. The problem was resolved when each of her groupmates broke off a Teddy Grahams™ leg and passed it over to Elizabeth.

"All those legs are as much as a whole one," said Elizabeth, satisfied.

Another group had two cookies remaining. These children polled each other about how old they were. I listened to Kelly's explanation.

"Everyone got 8 when we passed the plate around, but there were 2 left over. We decided that the kids who are 6 should let the kids who are 5 have the extra cookies. That was fair because Luke and Brett are 5."

I had to wonder, laughing to myself, what would have happened if 3 children at this table happed to be 5 years old! The group felt their plan was fair, so I gave them permission to eat their cookies.

As the lesson drew to a close, with some children quickly wolfing down their cookies and drifting off to play while others took a more sociable approach to enjoying a snack together, I had a lot to ponder. As I reflected on the thinking of the children and the many ways they dealt with the real-world problem and mathematical aspects of sharing cookies fairly, I was really glad that I had taken the risk of doing the lesson the way I did.

Looking Back . . .

Every time I reflect on this lesson, I am reminded of the power of rigorous, interesting problems to engage children's minds. First, I had expected to have to coax the children into thinking about the mathematics when we reread the story (and certainly not the first time I read it). Second, why didn't anyone eat the cookies? The ever-present cookies presented a temptation that even I hadn't been able to resist as I was putting them out on the plates. Why, then, didn't the children break the rule about not eating the cookies until the end? I think that the problem was more powerful than the draw of the sugar. (I have now used this book in succeeding years with similar results. The children become so immersed in the problem and trying out their solution strategies that they don't want to lose the problem by eating it.)

I had many questions going into the lesson. One was what would happen when the cookies didn't divide equally. Would the children be able to handle the mathematics this additional challenge presented? Another was the uneven number of cookies each group received, with some children thus receiving more cookies than others. (In actuality, no one has ever mentioned this.) It certainly would have been safer for me to have made sure the plates had equal amounts on them that could be divided equally. I was willing to take these risks because I thought the benefits of adding complexity to the problem outweighed the risks. I was reminded once again that if we want children to be risk takers, we need to be risk takers too.

About the Mathematics

The Doorbell Rang involves breaking a whole into equal parts and finding the number in each part. Thus, it deals with the concept of division. While few would think of teaching division to 5-year-olds, these children were exploring division in the context of fair shares, not learning the language and symbolism of division.

The children's mathematical reasoning was impressive. First, they made use of a rich set of computational strategies throughout, one example of which was the use of an additive approach to finding an answer, such as the number of cookies two children would get (6 + 6 = 12). This is a common approach among children. Children possess a wide range of strategies for computing, including counting on or back, doubling, and breaking numbers apart.

Another powerful example of mathematical reasoning occurred in the situation of Natalie's group struggling to find a fair way of sharing.

Since chocolate was of great value to Natalie, the children assigned a value of 2 to the chocolate cookies and a value of 1 to the vanilla cookies. Here, two does not refer to a number of things but is an arbitrary value assigned to a type of cookie, and "equal share" took on a new meaning. Two chocolate cookies and 1 vanilla cookie had the same value as 5 vanilla cookies. What made the two groups of cookies "equal" in the children's minds was not the number of cookies, but the value of them.

The children also were able to grasp the relationship between two quantities: the number of children and the number of cookies. They also understood the inverse relationship between these quantities, that is, as the number of children *increases*, the number of cookies per child *decreases*. Thus, they realized the number of cookies per child depended on the number of children. Experience with relationships that describe change is an important aspect of developing algebraic reasoning and the children did well with it.

Finally, we are forced to rethink what is appropriate mathematics for young children. Mathematical ideas often are withheld from children because the work goes beyond the expectations of what young children should investigate. Multiplication and division concepts, for example, are often viewed as not developmentally appropriate for young children and therefore are not introduced until later grades. We must rethink the mathematics in which children engage and what they can accomplish under a sense-making approach to learning. We must avoid the tendency to keep it simple because these are "little kids." Little kids really want big problems to solve, not simplicity!

The geometric and spatial knowledge children bring to school should be expanded by explorations, investigations, and discussions of shapes and structures in the classroom. Students should use their notions of geometric ideas to become more proficient in describing, representing, and navigating their environment.

  —Principles and Standards for School Mathematics (97)

4

November—It's Not Fair! They've Got More Blocks

Setting the Stage

The block-building center is important to me and I encourage my children to spend play time there. There is a great potential for geometric thinking and learning in working with unit blocks. However, it was now November and my teammate and I were less than happy with what was going on in the block area. In one of our weekly meetings we discussed the problems: we didn't see much evidence of shared work and the structures the children built were not becoming more complex. The children seemed to be in a block-building rut. The girls were working alone to build small structures, mainly as cages for toy animals, and the boys were working alone to make roads or ramps for their toy cars. We wondered how we could encourage our classes to collaborate more and do more sharing of ideas and discoveries with one another.

My teammate and I had adjoining classrooms with a folding door between them that we kept halfway open all the time. We decided to move our block-building areas closer together on the back wall, which increased the amount of space for building. More important, we hoped this new arrangement would encourage the children in each room to work together and collaborate on larger block structures. (See Figure 4–1.) Despite this redesign of the environment, my children continued to build the same kind of structures, although they occasionally observed one another's work. Eventually, my children began to work together. Roads became a bit more complex and buildings grew a little taller. This new level of activity led to the problem described here.

Block Shelves

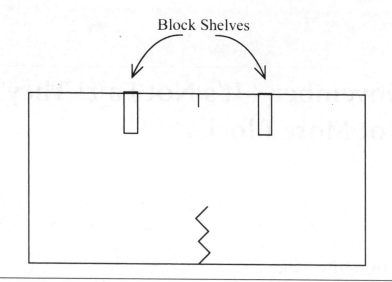

FIGURE 4–1   **Block Shelves**

The Lesson

The Problem

One day I overheard two children arguing. "It's no fair! Your class has more blocks than we do!"

"It's not true!" Kevin said. "We have the same!"

"No, you have more!" Raj insisted.

"Na-ah, you have just the same as us," Kevin countered.

Jenny, our class peacemaker, asked Raj, "Well, how do you know we have more?"

" 'Cause you can tell by looking!" answered Sean.

"Your buildings are much taller! You must have more blocks than us."

Jenny seemed convinced by this statement and asked me if our class did indeed have more blocks.

At first glance it seemed like a typical argument that young children engage in. On the other hand, I thought it could lead to productive problem solving. I knew that both classes had exactly the same number and kinds of block shapes. Further, my teammate and I had initialed each block for easy sorting and had even agreed on the exact same system for labeling our identical block shelves, which facilitated cleanup time. To encourage students to solve this dilemma for themselves, I decided that I would answer Jenny's question with one of my own. "I don't think so, Jenny," I commented, "but how could we find out for sure?"

As I had hoped, the children immediately got involved in the problem.

Getting Started

"We could check the initials," said Sean, referring to the markings on the two sets of blocks. "Maybe some of our blocks got on your side."

"We could count the blocks," Tony suggested.

"We could do both," Jenny said.

Several volunteers joined the project. They took every block off the shelves and checked the initials. They found that only one block was on the wrong side. The children had the blocks all over the floor and were just getting ready to count them when it was time to clean up. On top of that, Masyn shifted the discussion in a new direction.

"They won't fit back. There are too many now!" Masyn wailed.

Like many young children, Masyn thought there were many more blocks when they were spread all over the floor than when the same blocks were stacked neatly on the shelves. Even though he had helped take the blocks off the shelves, Masyn could not believe they would fit back on the shelves. I knew that telling him they would fit would not convince him. He had to convince himself.

"Let's try," I said in an encouraging voice.

Finally, the children did get the blocks back on the shelves. Then Tony said, "We'll have to count next time."

But I wondered to myself if there would be a "next time." It had taken these children their entire play time to do this task. Would they be interested enough to return to the problem the next day?

The Count Begins

Thank goodness, the next day at play time the same group headed to the block corner without hesitation and the counting process began. Everything started out fine, and then, just as I had predicted, they ran into trouble. Several children were counting the same blocks without a plan and kept losing count. The children couldn't remember which blocks had been counted, and as a result, some blocks were being counted twice. I thought briefly about intervening to suggest they organize the counting; however, I decided to let them proceed on their own and hopefully come to that conclusion for themselves, although I was not optimistic.

At this point Kevin took over. He assigned each child a particular type of block to count. Soon a group of children were scattered on the floor with chalkboards and chalk. He also systematized the counting and recording process. The child in charge of the half-unit rectangular blocks counted first, making tally marks on her chalkboard. The remaining children were fully engaged in helping her locate half-unit blocks. Then the children proceeded to the unit blocks and continued in that fashion.

The other class observed this, and soon the children from the other class were doing the same thing with their blocks. Finally, everything was moving smoothly. Both groups were fully engaged and I knew they

FIGURE 4–2   This child used functional spelling plus the universal representation for "no" to write "zero touches please!"

would have kept at it until they finished. But, as usual, cleanup time came too quickly. This led to another dilemma for the children (and their teacher). Since our kindergarten is half-day, we have a rule that blocks need to be put away at the end of play time as a courtesy to the other class. However, these children in the afternoon class were not finished with the counting task. Someone posed the question, "Can we leave the blocks out, just this once?"

I supported them. "I'll bet the morning class would agree to close this area until you finish your job, if I explain to them what you are doing." The children were delighted, but when I visited the area at the end of the day, someone had posted a sign to make sure the morning class got the message (see Figure 4–2).

The Counting Concludes

The next day the children went about completing their work. Jenny, who had finished her task of counting and tallying on her chalkboard, began to trace around a block, telling everyone that she was making a sign. After tracing around the block and cutting out the shape, she recorded the total number of that block inside of the drawing.

I asked Jenny to tell the other class about her idea of recording the results of the data collection. I asked her if she would like to show the information on the chart (see Figure 4–3). Soon other children worked with Jenny to transfer the information from the individual tallies to the chart.

When they were done, the two classes compared the results of their block counting. There were different amounts for only two shapes. The children in charge of those block shapes recounted. In one instance they discovered an error in counting blocks and in the other instance there was an error in counting tallies. Finally, both classes agreed that there were the same number of blocks on both sides.

FIGURE 4–3   Jenny's Chart

"You still have more than we do!" insisted Raj, ignoring the data the classes had spent so much time gathering.

"No we don't. We just build taller than you do!" Kevin countered. "See, we go up with our blocks and you build yours flat! That makes it look like we have more."

Raj seemed unconvinced, but the other children pondered this remark. At play time the next day, I noticed that the children were beginning to cross over to build with members of the other class. Soon they were collaborating on structures. Some days their structures were tall and on other days they built low structures that stretched across the room. There was increased discussion about what to build and how to go about building it. One day, I heard Raj say to Masyn, as they pushed cars along their block road, "Well it's nice to build tall sometimes, but roads don't go up!"

Looking Back . . .

As I reflect on this story, I realize that it illustrates two very different types of decisions that kindergarten teachers have to make: deliberate and

LOOKING
BACK

"on-the-spot." The first decision was the deliberate redesign of the kindergarten environment. I am constantly reevaluating the arrangement of my room and reflecting on ways of making the space more conducive to learning. I wanted to create a new arrangement of the space that would give the children more room for their block building, which, in turn, might expand their thinking about possible projects. I also felt that putting the two block areas in close proximity would encourage more collaboration between both classes. I made this decision jointly with my teammate, after we had brainstormed several plans and carefully considered the pros and cons of the new arrangement.

However, other kinds of decisions are tougher for me to make because they have to be made quickly, without much time for reflection. For instance, it would have been very easy to answer Jenny's initial question about whether we had more blocks. My answer would have diffused the argument and satisfied the children. Should I choose peace or an opportunity for learning? This may seem like a no-brainer. Of course teachers should offer opportunities for learning. However, on some days, restoring peace quickly is an alluring option!

Harder decisions involve when to step in and when to stand back and see what the children can do. This decision was relatively easy on the first day that the children "messed about" with the problem. However, when they proceeded in the same unorganized way on the second day, I thought more than briefly about helping them out. While I'm glad I didn't, I realize that if Kevin hadn't come to the rescue with his plan, I probably would have had to. Perhaps I would have asked, "How will you know that some blocks aren't being counted twice?" If they hadn't responded to that, I might have asked, "Have you thought about making a plan so that all the blocks are counted just once?" I might have even offered a suggestion about how to proceed. That day I didn't need to.

Most of my "on-the-spot" decisions come as a result of previous decisions I have made, as well as my confidence in the children's abilities to solve problems. Could I have made better decisions than I did? Perhaps. I chose the decisions that seemed most appropriate at the time, and knew that I would learn from them, realizing that none of them were earth-shaking. As I continue to work on developing a climate of reflection and sharing of ideas, missed opportunities can be explored further at another time.

About the Mathematics

The children's problem-solving approach is impressive. They engaged at a high level in all phases of the problem-solving process. Initially, they were involved in actions that are associated with *understanding the prob-*

lem. When their initial efforts were not productive, Kevin led the way in *devising a plan* to implement. This involved clarifying the task and creating an organized plan of attack. The children then *carried out the plan* in a systematic fashion. Finally, they engaged in *looking back* as they checked their results and dealt with errors.

Jennifer's way of representing the number of blocks should be noted. Children represent mathematical ideas in a variety of ways. At the most basic level, 22 blocks can be represented by drawing 22 rectangles, 1 rectangle for each block. The use of tally marks is somewhat more advanced. While 22 marks are still made, a tally, rather than a picture of a block, represents one block. Jennifer represented 22 blocks by writing "22" inside a single block. This is a big shift and shows a more advanced understanding of how a quantity can be represented. It was worthwhile to discuss her approach with the class and compare it to the other approaches. All children then had an opportunity to consider a new approach.

> Representing ideas and connecting the representations to mathematics lies at the heart of understanding mathematics. . . . Young students represent their mathematical ideas and procedures in many ways. They use physical objects such as their own fingers, natural language, drawings, diagrams, physical gestures, and symbols.
>
> —*Principles and Standards for School Mathematics* (136)

This problem-solving experience is set in the context of block-building activities. Block building has long held an important place in programs for young children and can be justified on several grounds. It is particularly important to note the mathematical significance of unit blocks. As children use them they explore important ideas about size and space, as well as informally explore measurement ideas of length, area, volume, and angles.

Unit blocks are constructed using a 1:2:4 ratio. The basic block is the unit rectangular prism. The other blocks are half the length of a unit block, twice the length of a unit block, and 4 times the length of a unit block. The same relationship holds for triangular prisms that are created by cutting the rectangular blocks along a diagonal. (See Figure 4–4.)

The design of the blocks permits children to explore relationships among them. Two half-unit blocks are equivalent to a unit block, and the longest block is the same as 4 unit blocks, 2 double-unit blocks, or 1 double-unit block and 2 unit blocks.

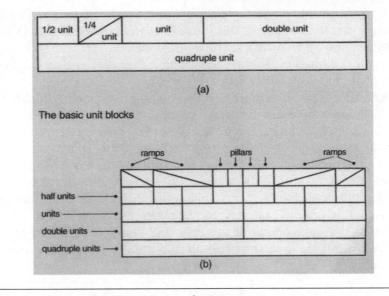

FIGURE 4–4   *Used with permission of NCTM.*

FIGURE 4–5   Later in the year, children try to solve the problem "How many possible combinations of blocks are the same length as 2 unit blocks placed end to end."

Instructional programs from prekindergarten through grade 12 should enable all students to analyze characteristics and properties of two- and three-dimensional geometric shapes and develop mathematical arguments about geometric relationships.

—Principles and Standards
for School Mathematics (96)

5

December—When Is a "Triangle" a Triangle?

Setting the Stage

My geometry lessons typically involve exploring ideas and learning about shapes as the children work with attribute blocks, pattern blocks, and geoboards. Two experiences in particular may have influenced the children's thinking in this lesson. Early in the year I had frequently emphasized that the sides of triangles don't have to be the same length and that no matter the position of the triangle it is still a triangle. In particular, one side doesn't have to be horizontal. The other experience, a play time activity, involved putting wooden blocks on the overhead projector and looking at the shapes that were projected. For example, the projection of a cylinder could be a circle or a rectangle, depending on how it is placed on the overhead.

In this lesson I decided to try something different. I planned to use a worksheet that I had been asked to evaluate that showed several drawings of real-world objects suggesting triangles and circles. I had some misgivings about using it, but I thought it could be a way to help the children review and clarify what they knew. The directions suggested that teachers discuss the page before handing it out. Although I couldn't envision a rich discussion resulting from this, I decided to give it a try.

I made an overhead transparency of one of the more appealing worksheets from the set. It showed children riding bicycles down the street of a town. The directions suggested having the children name some of the shapes in the picture. Then I would ask one of them to come to the overhead and outline a shape using an overhead pen. My expectation was that this would be a quick warm-up, taking about five minutes. Then I would hand out the worksheets for them to work on alone.

The Lesson

I stood next to my overhead projector and called the children to come and sit around it. I showed the scene that was depicted and discussed what was in it. Then I said, "Our job today is to find all the triangles in this picture. Who can find one?"

Many hands went up. A child came and outlined the pennant on the boy's bike (an isosceles triangle). Clearly this child didn't view a triangle as having three equal sides with one of them horizontal. Assuming the children understood the task, I was ready to move on to the next shape. However, the children stopped me. Their waving hands indicated they were enjoying doing the activity together and wanted to keep on going. So I called on a few more children. The next child outlined the top of the traffic light (an equilateral triangle). The triangle in the A on the pizza sign was outlined by another child. Then Cameron outlined a yield sign and called it an upside-down triangle.

What Is a Triangle?

"Does everybody agree that this is an upside-down triangle?" I asked.

"Oops!" Cameron said. "Triangles have three sides—they can go any direction. I just forgot." I was glad he remembered our emphasis on this earlier in the year when I had shown a triangle shape in many positions, each time asking, "Is this a triangle now?" I had wanted the children to know that position did not influence whether something was a triangle.

Another child came to outline a slice of pizza on a sign. I was ready to move on, so I asked, "Now, who can find a circle?"

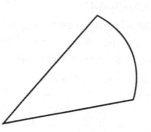

FIGURE 5-1   Pizza Slice

"Wait!" Elana's hand was up and waving. "There is another triangle!" She came up and outlined a shape that was the side of a traffic light. (See Figure 5-2.)

"Why do you say this is a triangle?" I asked.

"Because it has three corners," Elana replied.

I then realized that the worksheet had mixed drawings of triangles with real-world objects that resembled triangles, but were not triangles. I asked, "Does everyone agree that this is a triangle?"

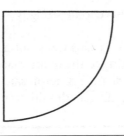

FIGURE 5–2   Traffic Light—Side View

Many children agreed, but some were uncertain.

"It has three corners but it doesn't really look like a triangle," Rachel said.

"Does anyone else think this isn't a triangle?" I asked.

"It really might not be a triangle," Kevin said. He came to the overhead and pointed to the shape. "This side [pointing to the curved side] looks like a half-moon shape. I don't think triangles look like this."

"Well," Starla said, "it has three sides. The pizza slice has that kind of side, too, and it's a triangle."

"Then I don't think it is a triangle, either," Kevin argued.

Oops—In my hurry to move along, I hadn't noticed that the pizza slice was not a triangle.

The children seem confused. Many thought Elana's shape was a triangle because it had three corners and three sides. Others were not sure.

"Well, what about that sign," said Cameron, pointing to the yield sign he had circled earlier. "It has curvy parts on the corners, too." (See Figure 5–3.)

FIGURE 5–3   Yield Sign

"Can triangles have curvy parts?" Elizabeth asked.

A discussion broke out among the children. It centered on whether triangles could have curvy parts and whether their corners had to be "pointy." I let them talk a bit while I gathered my thoughts and listened to theirs.

"Let me mention something else about triangles," I told them. "You were right that triangles must always have three corners and three sides, but the sides also have to be straight. Does this help you with this problem?"

"Oh, then I think the pizza slice is not a triangle and this one isn't, either," said Kevin, pointing to the quarter circle shape.

"Neither is the yield sign!" Cameron said.

"Three straight sides," Elizabeth said, to nobody in particular.

> Students need to see many examples of shapes that correspond to the same geometrical concept as well as a variety of shapes that are non-examples of the concept. For example, shapes that have a resemblance to triangles, but are not triangles.
>
> —*Principles and Standards for School Mathematics* (98)

What Is a Circle?

This was a very powerful discussion, much more valuable in my mind than having them complete the worksheet. I decided to continue the conversation with the class, asking whether anyone saw a circle. Hands shot up. The traffic lights, bike wheels, and pizza sign were quickly suggested. When one child mentioned the top of a topiary tree partially hidden by a sign, there was an outcry.

"That's not a circle!" Jenny said.

"Why not?" I asked.

"It doesn't go all the way around," Andy said.

"But it would be if that sign wasn't in the way," Michael argued. Most children were satisfied with this reasoning. One child still had a problem with Michael's answer.

"But the sides have wiggly parts. A circle can't have wiggly parts! It has to curve all around, smooth-like," Julian said.

"Julian, are you talking about the edge of a circle?" I asked, trying to provide a better word for what he was talking about.

"Yeah! The edge!" he said beaming. "It can't have no wiggly parts!"

"What about this?" I said, pointing to the chain wheel on the bike. "Is this a circle?"

"No," Elizabeth said. "It's sort of like a circle, but the edge goes in and out with lines. Circles can't have straight lines, I don't think."

"It may not be a circle, but it sure looks circular!" Michael said. This is the first time anyone had used this term to describe a shape, but from the children's nods I could tell that most of the children seemed to understand what Michael was saying. By "circular," he meant that it resembled a circle even though it was not a circle.

There was additional discussion when someone suggested that the dots on the girl's dress were too little to be circles. However, the class decided that size had nothing to do with shapes. Circles could be big or little, they decided, but they didn't have straight lines or bumps.

More About Circles—A Lot More

Just as I thought there was nothing more to be said about circles, the children proved me wrong. Jimmie was at the overhead, suggesting that the sausage slices on the pizza sign were circles. (See Figure 5–4.) But many children disagreed and Rachel was their spokesperson.

FIGURE 5–4   **View of Sausage Piece**

"These are more egg-shaped, like smooshed circles," she said. "Circles have to be round all around like balls. They don't have skinny parts."

In the drawing, the circular sausage slices were drawn as ovals. The first child may have been thinking of what the ovals *represented*, that is, circular slices of sausage, while the other children focused on the drawing itself.

After more circles were discovered, one child suggested the collar on the dog's neck, which appeared as a rectangle. My first thought was, "What is he thinking?"

"I need you to explain this to me," I said.

"Well, it looks like a rectangle now, but it's a collar and if you took it off and looked at it from the top, it would be a circle," Kevin explained. (See Figure 5–5.)

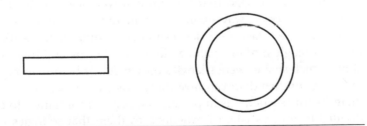

FIGURE 5–5   **Dog Collar—Side and Top Views**

My mind flashed back to the activities where the children looked at the projections from blocks placed on the overhead projector. If one looked at the dog's collar from the side it appeared like a rectangle in the drawing. But, the collar also suggested a cylindrical shape (without top or bottom) whose edge is a circle. This led to other interesting observations.

"Here's another circle!" said a child outlining the bike light. "If you look at it from the front." (See Figure 5–6.)

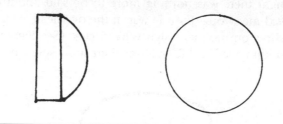

FIGURE 5–6   Bike Light—Side and Front Views

As the discussion continued, I reflected on the children's thinking. They were really thinking about the characteristics of shapes and forming some good ideas about them. I was amazed at the depth of this discussion. Because of the children's advanced understanding, I thought it would be good to have them take the worksheet home and talk to their parents about the shapes and our discussion about them. I also asked them to complete the page with their parents. They happily stuffed the page into their folders and prepared to go home.

"My mom's gonna think that sign is an upside-down triangle—I just know it!" Cameron said to me, smiling and shaking his head on the way out the door.

LOOKING BACK

Looking Back . . .

Cameron's comment made me laugh. *In fact,* I thought, *the way I was taught shapes in school, I might have called that yield sign an upside-down triangle myself!* I was glad that the children were learning to think about shapes in a deeper way—going beyond the "it's a triangle because it looks like one" stage to a deeper understanding of the attributes that make a triangle a triangle and a circle a circle. The children's confusion about which shapes were triangles presented a dilemma to me. I believe in letting children discover most things for themselves. However, I know there are times when it is important to present information to children. I decided to do this when I explained to them that triangles must have three straight sides. This was a missing piece of information that they needed in order to advance their conversation and their thinking about shapes. Knowing when and how to supply information that will move an idea forward is a tough call sometimes, but I think my decision this day was the right one.

I was impressed with the children's growing ability to have mathematical conversations. In September I was pleased that they were discussing mathematics, and now they were beginning to debate it! It was wonderful to hear the children analyzing and evaluating the ideas of others. Again I was reminded of the power of discourse that allows the knowledge of one child to become accessible to all children.

> Language, whether used to express ideas or to receive them, is a very powerful tool and should be used to foster the learning of mathematics. Communicating about mathematical ideas is a way for students to articulate, clarify, organize, and consolidate their thinking.
>
> —*Principles and Standards for School Mathematics* (128)

When children in my class explain ideas and hear similar ideas explained in different ways by other children who use slightly different language, they all form new insights and understandings.

About the Mathematics

The children's engagement in deep discourse about the characteristics of triangles and circles is impressive. It reminds us that young children find mathematical ideas interesting and enjoy reflecting on them. It also points out the pitfalls of poorly designed worksheets that can encourage mathematical misconceptions.

The lesson reminds us that developing an understanding of ideas is not always straightforward and that understanding is progressive, as there are multiple levels of complexity. The children brought a strong background knowledge about shapes to this lesson from their earlier classroom experiences. Thus, they *knew*, at least in a global sense, what a triangle is. They also knew that the lengths of sides and the position of a shape are not relevant. Yet the worksheet drawings forced them to reexamine what constitutes a triangle—not only three sides, but three straight sides, for example.

We also are reminded about the pitfalls in using real-world objects as exemplars of plane shapes. They can blur, for example, the distinction between a triangle (just the points that constitute the three straight sides) and a triangular region (the boundary plus the interior). A triangle formed from 3 thin sticks is a more appropriate model than a triangular region cut from construction paper. Real-world objects also cause us to distinguish between triangles and objects that resemble triangles but are not triangles. A yield sign and a pizza slice certainly seem like triangles, but they aren't triangles. It is preferable to ask children to find shapes that resemble or make them think of a triangle. In the lesson, Michael used the phrase "circular" to refer to this distinction. While "circular" isn't quite accurate, since "circular" and "triangular" are used to describe faces (i.e., regions) of three-dimensional objects, it was his way of communicating that the gear wheel resembled a circle.

Another complexity occurs when three-dimensional objects are drawn in two dimensions. Because of perspective, an object that resembles a circle, such as a slice of sausage on a pizza, can be drawn as an oval. Our eyes are trained to view it as circle-like. This may have led to the discussion in the lesson.

Teaching about shapes and their properties is not trivial; in fact, it can be complex. Thus, it is important that we have a clear understanding of the mathematics, so we can keep from reinforcing misconceptions even as we avoid becoming heavy-handed in our explanations and discussions. However, as this lesson teaches us, kindergartners are capable of going beyond global views about shapes to more sophisticated levels of interpretation.

Through their data investigations, young students should develop the idea that data, charts, and graphs give information. Teachers should encourage students to compare parts of the data and make statements about the data as a whole.

—*Principles and Standards for School Mathematics (113)*

6

January—Soup with Chicken Inside

Setting the Stage

This lesson grew out of my effort to make a mathematics-literature connection with *Stone Soup* (McGovern 1986), one of the books in our kindergarten program. My plan was to have the children represent on paper soup bowls the kind of soup served most often in their families. We would sort the bowls and then construct a graph of their data.

Over the years, I have learned a lot about increasing the effectiveness of work with graphing. For example, I now use fewer graphs but spend more time with each one, using the rule of thumb of devoting at least twice as much time to analyzing the data as it takes to make the graph. Also, when children make statements about the graph, I record their statements in speech bubbles and place them around the graph with the children's pictures on them. By this point in the year my class can deal with a four-category graph. More than that makes it too difficult for children to focus on relationships.

This lesson occurred in January. By then the children had had several in-depth experiences in graphing data and discussing the results. I have done this lesson for several years, but this time it took an unexpected turn. The children came up with 11 categories of soup, many more than the usual four categories. Fortunately, I was wise enough to turn the problem over to the children, which led to discussions and insights.

The Lesson

Collecting the Data

Today, the children were going to make stone soup. They had read and acted out *Stone Soup* several times prior to this, and now they were bringing the ingredients for the soup. I contributed a large smooth stone, the main ingredient. As the soup cooked, the children brainstormed all the different kinds of soups they had ever tasted, then I asked them to think of the kind of soup that they had *most often* at home. Asking for their favorite soup tends to put undue focus on the winning category. When this happens, children sometimes don't report their actual preference in their desire to fit in with the group.

I gave each child a soup bowl cutout and asked the children to draw or color the kind of soup served most often. As they worked, I walked around to see their responses and also to get a sense of what the categories might be for the graph. In previous years, there were generally four clear categories, but today was different. There were so many different varieties of soups represented in their drawings that I couldn't think of a way to reduce them to four categories. I finally decided that I would turn the problem over to the children and let them decide.

> Teachers should capitalize on unexpected learning opportunities. They should ask questions that direct students' thinking. . . .
>
> —*Principles and Standards for School Mathematics* (135)

Before doing that, I had the children come to the circle to discuss their drawings. Each child had an opportunity to talk about his or her soup. As they talked, I wrote each kind of soup on a chart and put a tally mark by it each time it was named (see Figure 6–1).

Grouping the Data

I wondered whether the children, who were used to organizing their data on the floor graph, would be able to draw meaningful information

Chicken and Stars	///
Tomato	///
Vegetable	///
Chicken and Rice	///
Chicken Noodleos	///
Cream of Broccoli	/
Minestrone	///
Chicken Noodle	///
Cream of Mushroom	/
Clam chowder (Manhattan)	/
ABC Soup	////

FIGURE 6–1   Soup Tally Chart

from this way of representing the data. So I asked, "What can you tell me by looking at the chart?"

Usually children's hands fly up and several suggestions are offered. Today, though, the children were quiet. Finally Prateek said, "There's too many ties." When I asked him to explain what he meant, he came to the chart and pointed to all the soups that had 3 votes. The rest of the children nodded, but no one else had anything to add.

This was a good point to introduce the problem that they would help me solve. I said, "I am trying to figure out a way to report our data on our floor graph. What do you think my problem is?"

The children were familiar with the four-column floor graph that we used to organize data.

One child offered, "There's too many kinds. They won't all fit."

I responded, "What can we do?"

"Well," Rachel said, "we could put all the chicken soups together."

"So I could make a label that says 'Chicken Soup'?" I asked.

"No," she replied. "It would have to say 'Soups with Chicken Inside.'" I wasn't clear why this was so important to her, but it was.

"Yeah," Brandon added. "Mine would go in there."

Nathan offered the next suggestion. "We could make a sign that says 'Soups with Vegetables Inside.'" Then he whispered to a friend sitting next to him, "Broccoli is a vegetable."

The discussion shifted to a new category. "We could make a sign that says 'Red Soup,'" said Delon, showing his tomato soup.

"Wait!" said Elle, pointing to her picture of vegetable soup. "That won't work because my soup is red *and* has vegetables inside it. We should make a label that says 'Tomato' for your soup," she told Delon. "The tomatoes make it red." Elle's statement reminded me of the work we had done earlier in the year with two-category Venn diagrams.

"Then my soup won't go anywhere!" wailed Stephen, who had drawn Manhattan clam chowder, which has a tomato base.

"Well," said the ever-practical Sharika, "you have to decide. Which is your soup—mostly red or mostly vegetable?" Her solution seemed to make sense to both Delon and Elle. Stephen also seemed satisfied with this plan.

I decided to summarize the work so far. "OK, we have decided on 3 labels: soups with chicken inside, soups with vegetables inside, and red soups—that is, soups with lots of tomato inside."

I wrote these labels on the chalkboard, eliciting help from the children with sounding out the words. Then I pointed to the fourth column on the graph and asked, "What about this column? What should we call it?"

I was expecting them to suggest "Other," as that is what we had often done. But Dan had another idea.

"'White Soup'—that's where I could put mine!" said Dan, holding up his cream of mushroom bowl.

I quickly placed the labels at the top of the columns and the children began to place their soup bowl drawings in the appropriate columns on the floor graph (see Figure 6–2). Some of the children discussed among themselves where their soup would go and soon everyone had made a decision. It was important for me not to impose my ideas about this. Perhaps Charlie's ABC soup did seem to him to have lots of vegetables in it, while Jill's ABC soup seemed to be mostly "red" to her.

Red Soup	Soup with Chicken Inside	Soup with Vegetables Inside	White Soup
7 bowls	12 bowls	8 bowls	1 bowl

FIGURE 6–2　Results of Class Survey

The children began to read the data, first focusing on the number in each category by counting. Carlene counted the "Soup with Chicken Inside" column, starting at one and counting each bowl. Paul counted this same column, but started where the vegetable and chicken columns were equal (8) and then counted on to 12. Charlie counted the vegetable column by twos. I was pleased to see three different counting strategies being used.

Next the children went beyond counting the number of soups in a category and looked for relationships between categories by comparing quantities. Again, interesting counting strategies were in evidence. Laura demonstrated how she counted back from 12 to 8 and found that there were 4 more bowls of chicken soup than vegetable soup. Joseph noted there was 1 less bowl of red soup than vegetable soup.

Going Beyond the Data

At this point, I let the children have time for free play while the soup continued to cook. Soon it was ready and the class sat down to enjoy their stone soup. As they were finishing up, one child asked when I was going to transfer the information from the floor graph to the door graph. "Not until the 'aftenoonies' do this activity," I said. "Then we'll combine the data."

My next question was, "What do you think will happen when they list the soup they have most often at home?"

The question led the children to a new level of analyzing data—predicting and inferring. They had to consider what the results of the data from both classes might be and how the overall totals might be affected. I used this opportunity to informally introduce some probability language. They determined that it was highly "unlikely" that the "White Soup" category would get the highest total when the data from both classes were combined. They also inferred that "Soup with Chicken Inside" would "probably" get the greatest total.

When I asked why they thought this, Joseph replied, "Because we put all the chicken soups together."

Matthew nicely summed up, "If you want people to like your soup, just put chicken in it!"

To highlight the mathematics and encourage prediction, I asked, "So, if you were a store owner, and you have very little space on your shelves for soup, which kinds would you put there?"

"Chicken!" the children chorused.

Extending the Lesson

"Now I have a homework job for you," I said. "Go home and ask your parents if you can sort your soups the way we did at school. Then let me know what happens."

Several children did this and brought back photos and drawings of their data collections. When revisiting the graph that displayed the combined data, I also asked the children to do a bit of research. I told them if they ever ate out in a restaurant, they should ask the server, "What is the soup du jour," explaining what the phrase meant. Both the children and their parents became very interested in the investigation. Reports began to come in. The children found that the soup of the day was usually one that contained chicken, or if there were two choices of soup, one of them contained chicken. We never did find a restaurant that offered two non-chicken soups. Even the parents began to research this and report to me. It seems that Matthew was right when he said, "If you want people to eat your soup, put chicken in it."

Looking Back . . .

As I look back, I am reminded how routine tasks can take some pretty interesting twists. Perhaps asking which soup was served most often rather than asking which soup was their favorite caused the number of varieties to be larger than usual. However, the 11 kinds of soup presented an interesting dilemma for me. I was glad I involved the children in determining the four categories for the graph. Putting the problem in their hands enabled them to take ownership of the work. I could tell they were proud of the categories they decided on—so proud that they insisted that I use their wording on the labels. While I am always a bit surprised by what they do when given these opportunities, I am seldom disappointed. They usually do far more than I think they can.

While unforeseen situations such as this one increase the complexity of my decision making, these unanticipated twists and turns keep teaching fresh for me.

About the Mathematics

Making graphs has become popular in most kindergarten classrooms. Making and discussing graphs is important, but graphs shouldn't exist by themselves. They also need to be set in the broader context of data analysis. Data analysis involves (a) formulating questions that can be addressed with data; (b) collecting, organizing, and displaying the data; (c) looking for patterns and relationships in the data; and (d) making conjectures and predictions based on the data. This lesson clearly indicates that kindergarten children are not too young to have informal experiences with data investigations.

The lesson centered on problems of sorting or organizing data. As the lesson indicates, this is not always simple, as in the case of a piece of data that fits two categories. The children's solution was a practical one that worked fine for them. A second problem was devising ways of representing the data. Previous to this experience, making a graph was the primary way of representing data. There were two types of graphs, a floor graph on which objects could be placed, and a graph located on the door to which data was transferred. A new way of representing data—using a chart or table—was introduced.

Third, the children described and analyzed the data in various ways. They began by focusing on the number of items in each category. Then they shifted to making comparisons between pieces of data, such as "There are four more chicken soups than red soups." Finally, the children made informal predictions about what would happen when the data from the afternoon class was joined with their data.

The lesson captures the mathematical richness of embedding graphing experiences within an investigation in data analysis. The level of engagement and the quality of the children's thinking suggest that this is appropriate and enjoyable for young learners.

Developing mathematical reasoning is a part of learning mathematics. In this lesson children used a variety of counting strategies. At the beginning of kindergarten most children count all objects by ones. They also make comparisons by using basic counting. A key goal for kindergarten teachers is to help children begin to move to more mature ways of counting and comparing quantities.

> Mathematics teaching in the lower grades should encourage students' strategies and build on them as ways of developing more general ideas and systematic approaches.
>
> —*Principles and Standards for School Mathematics* (76)

Charlie used a more advanced method, counting by twos. When comparing the number of entries for chicken and vegetable soups, Laura *counted back* from 12 to 8 to find there were 4 more bowls of chicken soup, while Paul found the place where the two columns were the same height and *counted on* 4 to get to 12. As teachers we need to be reminded that children develop skills in a variety of settings. We also need to be aware of the strategies that children use. It is important to highlight these strategies when they occur and discuss them with the whole class.

In prekindergarten through grade 2, mathematical concepts develop at different times and rates for each child. . . . All students need adequate time and opportunity to develop, construct, test, and reflect on their increasing understanding of mathematics.

*—Principles and Standards
for School Mathematics (76)*

7

February—The Secret of the Hearts

Setting the Stage

It was about time for our annual 100-Day celebration to occur. This event marks the 100th day of school and provides an opportunity to highlight 100 as an important benchmark number. The children had brought in their collections of 100 objects—buttons, stamps, etc. I used their collections to design six activities for the children to do over several days. Each basket activity provided opportunities for children to work together on an important mathematical idea. One activity involved finding the heaviest of three collections by weighing two of them at a time. In another activity children chose a collection and then grouped the objects by ten to find whether the collection had 100 objects (some had more and some had less). This story involves graphing collections of 100 objects.

My plan was to allow two weeks for the children to work on the six activities. This story focuses on the work of one group of students over several days with the graphing activity. The children had chosen a collection of 100 candy conversations hearts to graph using a grid that had been taped to the table. This lesson focuses on two dilemmas I faced. One was letting children choose the tasks they worked on, rather than assigning them to particular activities each day. A question by another teacher was causing me to rethink my practice of letting them choose the tasks they work on. The teacher had noted that letting children choose might mean that some children would not complete all the basket activities and thus miss something important. I still believed that it is important for children to make their own choices, and I preferred observing and interacting with children over keeping extensive records. However, I still questioned myself a bit.

Because the work of the graphing group was so interesting, I chose to spend the majority of my the time with these children. This was the second dilemma. Spending a lot of time with one group meant devoting less attention to the work of the other groups and perhaps missing interesting or important events.

The Story

My kindergarten class was eager to begin working again with our 100 Collections math baskets. While the table captains delivered the baskets to the designated areas, I asked the children to think about the activity they would find interesting to work with today. After the children chatted about where they wanted to go, they were ready to proceed.

I asked, "Since today is Thursday, who gets to make first choices today?"

"Greens!" was the enthusiastic response of the children with green name tags.

They moved quickly to their chosen baskets, with the rest of the children taking their turn in the rotation order we used. Within a minute or two, all the children had begun to work. I began moving about the room, observing the work. Richard, Tommy, Ryan, and Rebecca had chosen to work at the Graphing Basket. When I walked by the table, they had placed only 5 or 6 candy hearts on the graph.

A Conflict Emerges

Tommy looked up at me and said, "Rebecca says the yellows are going to win, but she's wrong."

"Rebecca, why do you say the yellow hearts will make the longest column?" I asked, replacing "win" with a more mathematical term.

Rebecca, a rather quiet and shy child, replied in a soft voice, "Because yesterday I did the hearts and the yellows made the longest."

Her answer made perfect sense to me, but not to the boys. "Well, today that's not gonna happen because look—there's hardly no yellows!" Ryan said as he pointed to hearts on the graph.

The other boys nodded in agreement at this statement. Rebecca looked uncertain. Lots of thoughts went through my mind:

> *If Rebecca did this activity yesterday, why did Ryan's statement make more sense to the boys than Rebecca's experience? Were the boys more willing to listen to Ryan because he was a boy? Was Rebecca's uncertainty due to her stage of development or a lack of confidence in herself as a learner? Did the fact that the group was mostly boys affect her confidence? Or were there other factors that caused the boys' views?*

"Do you have all the hearts graphed yet?" I asked.

"No, not yet, but it's still not going to win," Ryan replied.

"Well, why not put a few more down and then see what you think," I suggested. I took a few steps away from the table, quickly scanning the room to be sure the other groups were engaged.

Several thoughts went running through my head.

Should I spend this much time with this group? I really felt that these children's mathematical dilemma required my attention. If I didn't stay they might go to another table and I was not willing to let that happen, especially when important mathematical questions needed to be answered here. My attention and interest would probably keep them going. On the other hand, what was I missing? What were the other 22 children in my class doing? Were there other children who need my attention just as much?

Rebecca Under Attack

I turned my attention back to the hearts group. I noticed that the children had decided on a fair way to place hearts on the graph. Each child took one heart out of the bag, then passed it to the next person. However, I also noticed that "winning" had become the focus of this activity for the boys, who each chose a purple heart to place on the grid, while Rebecca continued to choose a yellow heart each time. Since there were more boys, the purple heart column continued to grow.

"See! We told you, Rebecca!" Tommy crowed.

Rebecca seemed very puzzled by this turn of events, and I noticed her body begin to turn away from the table.

Inwardly, I could feel myself getting upset with the boys. Was I overreacting to the gender equity issues and to situations where girls may not feel comfortable? Why did the boys always have to make everything a competition? Were they ganging up on Rebecca? Then I thought to myself, "Maybe they didn't mean any harm." Yet, perhaps if there were another girl in this group, Rebecca would feel more comfortable. I wondered again if I should structure math activities so that there were an equal number of boys and girls. But if I did this it would conflict with my desire for the children to choose their own activities.

I focused my attention on Rebecca, who clearly was not happy.

My heart went out to this shy child, who was unsure of herself in so many situations. What would happen if she left the group now? Nothing positive, I was sure, and I was determined not to let that happen. How might I keep her engaged? Should I side openly with her against the boys? How could I keep Rebecca from leaving and refocus the children on the activity?

"What about the rest of the bag? Are you going to put them all out?" I asked. The children silently began passing the bag again. Rebecca stayed. When it was Richard's turn, he spoke up.

"Hey look, there's lots of yellow still in there," he said, pointing to the bag.

"Don't put them down!" Tommy yelled as he jumped up and down, trying to grab the bag out of Richard's hands,

"We have to put them down," Ryan said, "or it won't be fair."

"OK, but the purples are still going to be the winner!" Tommy said.

I was glad that Richard and Ryan were beginning to focus on the remaining contents of the bag. Should I say something to help Tommy do so too? I decided to use his vocabulary to describe the problem.

"Tommy, why do you suppose the yellow hearts were the winners yesterday?" I asked.

"Because they put yellow in this column, maybe," he replied, quickly pointing to the column in which the purple hearts were today.

This reasoning, which always surprises me, makes perfect sense to immature learners like Tommy who fail to consider that the number of hearts and the number of each color remain constant from day to day. Tommy seemed perfectly comfortable with his theory, so I didn't think it would be helpful to question or correct it. Suppressing a smile, I looked at the other children to see if they agreed.

Richard spoke up again. "No, that wouldn't matter, Tommy. It wouldn't make any difference where she put them. There would be the same number of hearts."

This comment seemed to confuse Ryan. After a moment, he asked Rebecca, "Are you sure the yellows won yesterday?" A hesitant Rebecca nodded yes.

"Then I think they might be the winners today, too," Ryan said.

"No way!" Tommy said.

"Yes way, because look. Nobody put any more hearts in the bag last night. It's the same hearts," Ryan explained.

Richard nodded in agreement as he took the next turn. The children continued to pass the bag around, but Ryan began to help Rebecca by choosing a yellow heart. Richard closed his eyes each time and drew a heart randomly, but Tommy chose purple hearts until they were all gone. Then he chose other colors, avoiding the yellows. When the hearts were all placed in the appropriate columns, Rebecca's face lit up.

"See, I told you so!" she crowed.

Tommy looked shocked and said, "How could that happen? You cheated!" Then he paused and asked, "Did you cheat?"

Tommy's reactions of disbelief, accusation, and then questioning were fascinating to me. Since the results made no sense to him, he began to formulate possibilities, including magic and trickery as reasonable hypotheses. When he formed the *question* about cheating after the *accusa-*

tion of cheating, I realized that he was sincerely trying to figure out what happened. (I have often observed children call others "cheaters" when they are trying to make sense of outcomes and events.) I sensed that Richard and Ryan did not share Tommy's confusion, nor did they question Rebecca's actions. Rebecca, however, did seem confused, embarrassed . . . and a little guilty.

> *Did she think she had done something unfair to cause the yellow hearts to "win"? How could I convince her that she hadn't?*

A Tentative Resolution

I decided to sidestep the cheating issue for now, hoping to refocus Rebecca's and Tommy's thinking. I interjected a question at this point, making one more attempt to eliminate the word *win* from the activity.

"I wonder what did happen? Why did the yellow hearts have the longest column both days?" I asked.

Richard answered quickly. "Because nobody changed the hearts— they have the same number."

"And what would happen if we graphed these hearts again tomorrow?" I asked.

Rebecca and Tommy looked uncertain, but Ryan and Richard said in unison, "The same thing!"

Suddenly Tommy's face brightened. He began to march around the table, chanting, "We know the secret of the hearts! We know the secret of the hearts!"

I wasn't convinced that Tommy really "knew the secret" at all, but he seemed genuinely pleased with himself as the other children followed him around the table, echoing his chant.

The next day, Tommy, Rebecca, and Ryan repeated the activity, while Richard chose to move to another activity. The third day, Ryan left the group to try another basket, but Tommy and Rebecca continued to work at graphing the hearts for several more days. As they worked, sometimes alone and sometimes alongside other children, they grew more confident that the yellows would "win." They conferred together about which column they would put the yellow hearts in each day, testing Tommy's hypothesis that position might affect the results. Later they tested Rebecca's hypothesis that always choosing a certain color from the bag might make it win. Eventually, they chose another 100 collection to graph, this time colored rings, and finally I noticed that they were counting the number of objects in each column. Occasionally they made a counting error, but they seemed so absorbed in their work, I didn't interfere. Toward the end of the month, most of the children in class had spent some time at every basket (although I had no chart to prove it), but Rebecca and Tommy stayed at yellow table, inviting others to join their "graph club."

Looking Back . . .

As I reflected on this series of incidents, I was glad that I had chosen to focus my observations on this group's work. If I had balanced my time between all the groups on this day, I would not have noticed all the subtleties of the experience. For instance, I might not have observed the manner in which the children were carefully choosing which hearts to place on the graph and the reasons behind those choices. Actually, in this case, without my physical presence, the work itself might have disintegrated. Rebecca would probably have moved away, leaving with a bad taste in her mouth about the experience and a diminished view of herself as a mathematician. The boys may or may not have continued this activity. If they had continued, it would have been without the level of insight that came about as a result of the questions I was able to pose because I had been there to observe the situation. Perhaps I missed other things that were going on in the classroom, but I really felt I got to know these four children as learners.

I really believe that the most effective assessment tools are the eyes and ears of the teacher. However, when I concentrate this hard on observing and interacting with children, I find I am not able to use whole-class recording sheets very effectively. This is a dilemma for me in this age of "accountability." I do think it is very important to record what is going on in my classroom. However, this experience taught me the value of focusing on a few children at a time and trusting myself to remember these observations later as I write in my computer journal. Looking back, I saw that I could let the children help me with record keeping. In the future, I decided, I would post a chart where they could record their names by "The Most Interesting Math Basket I Visited Today." (Allowing them to record only one choice would keep them from "basket hopping" in order to have the most visits recorded on this chart.)

Letting children make choices is another practice that is often called into question. However, as I thought back to Rebecca and Tommy, I wondered what would have happened if they had been asked to go to a different math basket the next day. While it took these two learners longer than one might expect to understand that the number of candy hearts would remain constant, no matter where they were placed or in what order, I felt this was an important concept for them to learn. The fact that they both continued to choose this math basket is evidence that they thought so, too! Ryan and Richard also had the choice to move on after they had made sense of the situation. What if they had been forced to return to this math basket because it was their "turn"? This incident strengthened my belief in young children's right to make decisions about their learning.

About the Mathematics

It is difficult to separate the mathematics of a lesson from the learning of that mathematics. While we can't ignore the mathematics, so often teaching involves far more than mathematics. In this case the graphing task was straightforward; graphing the same objects from one day to the next meant the number of each kind would be the same. Yet, what is logically obvious to adults is not necessarily obvious to children.

It was clear that Rebecca and Tommy needed time and repeated experiences to convince themselves of the results. Throughout, they quite systematically tested a series of hypotheses until finally they reached the conclusion that Richard and Ryan arrived at several days earlier.

> Because young children develop a disposition for mathematics from their early experiences, opportunities for learning should be positive and supportive. Children must learn to trust their own abilities to make sense of mathematics.
>
> —*Principles and Standards for School Mathematics* (74)

If we want students to make sense of mathematics—that is, to have a deep understanding of mathematical concepts and relationships—we must provide the time and experiences that they need. Less mature and less confident children don't have to experience failure in mathematics. Rather, they can be successful if we are sensitive to their needs.

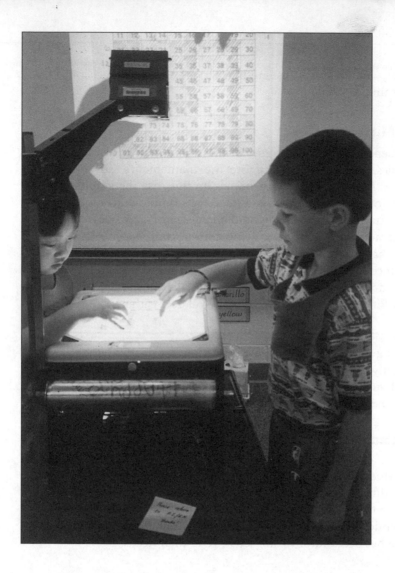

Preschoolers recognize patterns in their environment and, through experiences in school, should become more skilled in noticing patterns in arrangements of objects, shapes, and numbers and in using patterns to predict what comes next in an arrangement.

—*Principles and Standards for School Mathematics (91)*

8

March—Ms. McGill's Challenge

Setting the Stage

Teaching children to form numerals has always been troublesome for me. It's not that it is unimportant, for it *is* important. For one thing, it's an aspect of mathematical representation, that is, representing quantities symbolically. What bothers me is taking math time to do it. I want math time to be devoted to getting children to work with mathematical ideas, develop reasoning, solve problems, find patterns, and share their thinking with one another.

Over the years I have found that it is better to delay formal instruction in writing numerals until later in the year when children have more fine motor control. It goes more smoothly and children are more successful. So I delay it until the end of February or the beginning of March and devote 10 days to it, one day for each number from 1 to 10. I also have tried to include some meaningful mathematics in the work, but I wasn't satisfied that the work was as mathematically productive as it could be.

I was still searching for a better way to do it—an approach that would engage them and encourage them to do their best. After much thought a plan hit me—why not present the work in the form of a challenge? I present challenges throughout the year. Sometimes they come from my husband, and sometimes from the "Super Nintendos" of school (our school superintendent). This time it would come from the principal, even though she was initially unaware of her challenge. I would tie the work into writing numbers to 100, the use of the hundreds chart, and investigating patterns. As a result, children would write numbers beyond 10, although that was not the primary goal. The basic goal remained learning to form the numerals 0 through 9.

The Lesson

A Challenge Is Posed

The children looked up at me, anticipating the beginning of math time. I explained to the class that Ms. McGill, the school principal, had issued a challenge to them and that it was really hard. Their ears perked up when I said the challenge was to learn to write all the numbers to 100 by the end of March (about $3\frac{1}{2}$ weeks away). Some children made faces and a few groaned. This would be hard and maybe unattainable.

"Did you accept the challenge?" Travis asked quietly.

"Of course, she did! She always does!" Aaron said. His eyes were gleaming. Aaron is a very capable child and he may have even seen the "joke" of this challenge.

"Don't worry, children," I said, "I'll show you how to do it the easy way. Whenever a job is just too big, the secret is to start at the beginning and think small. Today we'll learn how to write a 1." I showed them how to form the numeral and had them practice making it. Then I asked how many numbers they now knew how to write. Several children responded "One" in chorus. I paused and focused my eyes on the hundreds chart that was posted in the room. (See Figure 8–1.)

"Is that all?" I asked and paused. One of the children pointed to the hundreds chart and said we could also write 11. "Now let's see, class. How many numbers do we know how to write?" They saw that they

Hundreds Chart

1	2	3	4	5	6	7	8	9	10
11	12	13	14	15	16	17	18	19	20
21	22	23	24	25	26	27	28	29	30
31	32	33	34	35	36	37	38	39	40
41	42	43	44	45	46	47	48	49	50
51	52	53	54	55	56	57	58	59	60
61	62	63	64	65	66	67	68	69	70
71	72	73	74	75	76	77	78	79	80
81	82	83	84	85	86	87	88	89	90
91	92	93	94	95	96	97	98	99	100

FIGURE 8–1   Hundreds Chart

could write 1 and 11 and I shaded these numbers on the hundreds chart. (See Figure 8–2, Day One).

Travis noted with frustration on his face, "But that's only two numbers. We'll never get to 100 in one month."

Aaron quickly jumped into the conversation. "Oh yes we will!" he crowed. "Just wait." I think he had seen the plan I had devised.

As the lesson began the next day, Kristen blurted out, "98 more to go."

After demonstrating the proper way to form a 2 and having them try it, I asked the children to tell me the new numbers we could write now. They looked at the hundreds chart and several children called out 2, 22, 21, and 12. (See Figure 8–2, Day Two.)

"That's four more!" Timmy said. "Now we know 6."

The next day, before I demonstrated how to form a 3, I asked the children to predict how many new numbers they would be able to write when they learned how to write 3. While they could name some of the numbers, they could not identify all six of them. I shaded the six new numbers on the hundreds chart. (See Figure 8–2, Day Three.) Now the following numbers were shaded: 1, 2, 3, 11, 12, 13, 21, 22, 23, 31, 32, and 33.

"That's 12 now!" Jeff said. "We still have a long way to go."

"When do you think we will be halfway there?" I asked.

"I think maybe when we can make 5 cause 5 is half of 10," Jenny said. That prediction was not correct, but it certainly was good thinking on her part and a plausible prediction.

"I don't think so. We're already at 3 now and only have 12 numbers . . . and 5 is just two numbers away," Kristen said. That seemed like another good argument to me.

I responded, "Let's think about that one. Today when you are finished your practice page, turn it over and make a prediction about how many numbers we will be able to write tomorrow when we know how to make a 4."

Most of the children accepted this challenge, but Katie said, "I'm not so good at making predictions about numbers." That worried me, for I had seen Katie struggle to follow some of the reasoning in the class and I

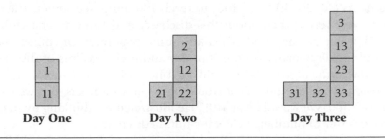

Day One   **Day Two**   **Day Three**

FIGURE 8–2   Days One, Two, and Three

didn't want her to develop the attitude that she wasn't good at math. I asked her to come with me to my desk.

I said, "Katie, you are good at numbers, but part of your brain is trying to tell you that you're not. I'm going to help you see that you are. Do you remember how many numbers we can make after today?" Katie remembered that it was 12.

"Good memory! Now, do you think we will know how to make more numbers or fewer numbers tomorrow?"

"More," Katie said.

"Right! Do you think it will be a lot more or just a few more?" I asked.

"Oh, just a few more," came her confident reply.

"Can you think of a number that is just a few more than 12?" Katie thought of 15 and wrote this number on her page. Her face beamed as I overheard her say to a friend, "I think it will be about 15," and then explain her reasoning.

Patterns and Predictions

On the fifth day, the children were surprised to learn that they were not halfway to 100 and they were a little disappointed. Still, they persevered. Each day the excitement built as the children tried to predict how many new numbers they would be able to write.

On the eighth day, Jeff said he saw a pattern. "On the first day we learned 2 new numbers, on the second day we learned 4, and on the third day we learned 6 new numbers." He went on to recount the new numbers added each day. "I think it will always be two more new numbers each day than the day before." He went to the overhead projector to show his pattern. (See Figure 8–3.)

The other children—and their teacher—studied this pattern. "So you are predicting that we will be able to make 16 today," I said.

"Yep!" Jeff said. We checked and he was correct.

Then Claire spoke up. "So tomorrow it will be 18 new numbers and the next day it will be 20!"

I could see that on the 10th day we would only need to write 10 new numbers (10, 20, 30, . . . , 100) to reach 100, but I kept quiet. The children were very excited about this discovery and I saw several children check it out on the hundreds chart during play time. Of course, Aaron found the discrepancy on the 10th day and there was lots of discussion about why the pattern didn't hold. No one could quite figure it out.

Finally Aaron said, "That would be 20 new numbers, but we would be over 100. We would be at 110!" He illustrated his thinking by making an extra row of numbers below the hundreds chart.

"Let's don't do 110!" Travis said. "It's too hard. Besides, the challenge was only to 100."

Hundreds Chart

1	2	3	4	5	6	7	8	9	10
11	12	13	14	15	16	17	18	19	20
21	22	23	24	25	26	27	28	29	30
31	32	33	34	35	36	37	38	39	40
41	42	43	44	45	46	47	48	49	50
51	52	53	54	55	56	57	58	59	60
61	62	63	64	65	66	67	68	69	70
71	72	73	74	75	76	77	78	79	80
81	82	83	84	85	86	87	88	89	90
91	92	93	94	95	96	97	98	99	100

FIGURE 8–3   Growing Pattern on 100 Chart

The next day, the children were so exited because they could now write all the numbers to 100. We had Ms. McGill come to check on our progress and she was properly impressed with their efforts. Nylah was proud to also share another discovery the class had made. "Actually, Ms. Gill, we can also write numbers higher than 100," she said. Nylah demonstrated how to make 151. The children were amazed, but soon they began to call out other numbers that were greater than 100 for Nylah to write on the chalkboard. I could tell by their faces that they had experienced a feeling of mathematical power and insight.

A New Challenge and a New Problem

As Nylah was talking, I was taking a mental break. I had been fascinated to watch how a simple hundreds chart transparency had caused so much excitement and learning. In my mind I was planning a way to bring closure to this work when I heard Ms. McGill give the children a new challenge: writing all the letters necessary to write every word in the English language before the end of the year!

They gasped—and so did I! Ms. McGill knew that letter formation was next on the handwriting agenda, but there was no way I could apply the numeral-writing approach to letters. The big smile on her face made it clear that she was greatly enjoying the moment. There was lots of excited talking when I told the principal we would accept her challenge. When she left, I told the children in a conspiratorial fashion, "I know a secret. That's not so many letters. We only have to learn 26!" There were sighs of relief from the children and we were ready to move on.

But Nylah said, "Actually, that's not exactly true. It would really be 52."

"Why?" I asked. I should have known I would be challenged on the number of letters.

"Because we would have to learn the upper- and lowercase and there are 26 letters. 26 + 26 = 52," she replied.

"How do you know that 26 + 26 is 52?" I inquired.

Nylah wasn't sure, but she thought her dad had told her that.

"How can we figure out if Nylah's dad is right?" I asked the children, writing "26 + 26" horizontally on the chalkboard. I have learned that the horizontal format encourages children to think it through, rather than just use the traditional rules for adding two-digit numbers.

"I can do that!" Richard offered. "See, I know that 20 + 20 = 40. And I know that 6 + 6 = 12." At this point he seemed unsure of what to do next. So I asked the other children what they thought Richard could do next.

"Well," Kristen said, "I took the 40 and then I took the 12 and I added them." She came to the board and added 40 and 12 vertically. She seemed to understand what she was doing, but other children seemed confused by this. I asked for other suggestions.

Jeff responded, "I knew that 20 + 20 was 40. That left the 6 + 6. I knew that 5 + 5 = 10. I added this 10 to the 40 to get 50. Then I added the 2 left over to it and that was 52." Jeff used his fingers to illustrate his point as he talked. He pointed out that 6 is 1 more than 5 so 6 and 6 is two more than 5 and 5.

"Does that seem reasonable?" I asked.

"Yeah," answered several children in the group.

I knew that some children in my class did not follow this line of thinking, nor should they have. I had a broad range of abilities in this class. I wanted to affirm those who had participated without making the rest of the class feel badly. What could I teach with my praise?

I said, "Everyone who contributed to solving this problem by talking, please stand." Several students stood up. "Now, everyone who contributed to solving this problem by listening, please stand." The rest of the students stood.

Then I said, "Please give these children who are standing up a hand. It is important to know that good mathematicians talk about their ideas with others and listen to other people's ideas, too, even if they don't always understand the ideas."

LOOKING BACK | Looking Back . . .

This series of lessons certainly differs from the way I usually present mathematics to my class. I prefer to connect mathematical ideas to a real-world context. These lessons, however, were rather routine and devoted to a specific skill—that of learning to form numerals. I *did* want to help my students develop the important skill of forming these standard mathematical symbols as tools to represent their thinking. However, I must admit that I find drill-and-skill work boring to teach. If it was boring for me, how was I going to make it interesting for my class?

Thinking back, I was delighted to see that my idea *was* interesting to them. In fact, the class seemed to treat this lesson like any other math lesson—as a problem to be solved—and they participated enthusiastically. And, while the children did learn to write numerals, they also engaged in some very powerful mathematical reasoning. I was glad to see that the children expected to find patterns in their work. This confirmed to me that the children were beginning to connect the foundational pattern work we had done with shapes and colors to the base ten number system.

When the additional challenge of figuring out how many letters we would need to form was presented, the children seemed to *expect* that they could solve it. Many contributed a piece of knowledge and helped move the work forward. Others were working hard to listen and understand the ideas of their classmates. It was clear to me that this class had really become a community of learners, working together to make sense of mathematics.

About the Mathematics

This story highlights two powerful aspects of mathematics. First, there is the central role that number patterns played in the work. Jeff noticed that "it will always be two more new numbers each day than the day before." He saw that there was a constant increase of two (see Figure 8–4). This pattern allowed the children to predict with confidence that 16 new numbers would be written on the eighth day.

There is also a second pattern that Angela and the children discussed later. It deals with the *total* number of numerals written each day and is an example of a growth pattern. The total number of numbers grows from 2 on the first day, to 6 on the second day (a gain of 4), to 12 (a gain of 6), to 20 (a gain of 8), etc. Rather than the amount of change being constant, it grows by 2 each time.

It is very important that kindergarten children's work with color and shape patterns be extended to number patterns. Too often, number patterns are neglected. Examining and discussing the characteristics of number patterns is a part of algebraic reasoning and this lesson is a first step in building a foundation for later work with algebraic ideas.

The second example is the children's thinking for adding 26 and 26. Jeff's computational strategy was based on decomposing 26 into 20 and 6. His thinking was accepted by the class, possibly because the word name (twenty-six) suggests the two parts. The next step was to add the

Day	Number of New Numbers written	Day	Cummulative Total
Day 1	2	Day 1	2
Day 2	4	Day 2	6
Day 3	6	Day 3	12
Day 4	8	Day 4	20

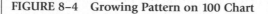

FIGURE 8–4   Growing Pattern on 100 Chart

two 20s (20 + 20) and then add the two 6s (6 + 6). The four "parts" were combined in a way that made sense to the children.

Finding 20 + 20 was easy because of its connection to 2 + 2. For 6 + 6, some children just knew that 6 and 6 is 12. They then had to add 40 and 12 to find the sum of 26 and 26. Jeff used 5 + 5. He added 10 (the sum of 5 and 5) to 40 and then added the "leftover 2" to 50 and got 52.

Adults are often surprised by children's ability to invent insightful ways of computing with larger numbers. For most children, this thinking is natural and is a product of their number sense. Not only does this work enable them to learn the highly useful skill of mental computation, it eventually leads to learning written computation without difficulty.

> When students compute with strategies they invent or choose because they are meaningful, their learning tends to be robust—they are able to remember and apply their knowledge.
>
> —*Principles and Standards for School Mathematics* (86)

By learning problem solving in mathematics, students should acquire ways of thinking, habits of persistence and curiosity, and confidence in unfamiliar situations that will serve them well outside the mathematics classroom.

  —Principles and Standards for School Mathematics (52)

9

April—Aaron and the Tall Tower

Setting the Stage

Good mathematics arises from many settings—a classroom event, a problem that is posed, a children's book, a planned lesson. A child's comment during play time can also launch a major investigation. The following investigation was the result of a comment one child made during our daily play time. It was one of those times when I happened to be at the right place at the right time with the right questions.

The problem centers on the use of Solo® cups for building towers. These colorful cups have had a large place in my classroom play for over 15 years as children have enjoyed building and patterning with them. Every year the children use the cups differently. Some years they tend to make patterns and letters and construct mazes. This year my class was into tower building. They accomplished this by turning the cups upside down and stacking them. The children were particularly interested in seeing how high they could stack the cups. The day before this lesson, they had made a pyramid-shaped structure that was 17 rows tall. Now they were trying build even higher and set a new record.

Let me introduce you to the children's tower-building techniques. Typically, they would begin building a tower by placing a number of cups in a row and then building up. Each row had one fewer cup than the one below it. (See Figure 9–1.)

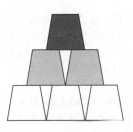

FIGURE 9–1

Once the children had made a tower, they had an interesting technique for making it taller. They would put an extra cup at one end of each row and one cup on the top. (See Figure 9–2.) This is a very workable and efficient process that resulted in stable towers that didn't topple over. This tower-building approach was at the heart of the events that unfold here.

FIGURE 9–2

The Investigation

The tower builders were at it again, trying to go beyond their efforts of the previous day. But today they did something new. The children started out with a long strip of cups and were building on it. There must have been 6 children working on it in a very organized way, which is why the row approach worked out.

Aaron Speaks Out

"It's gonna be 32 rows tall," one of the children predicted.

My ears perked up and I turned to see who spoke. It was Aaron, a talented mathematics student who was not even involved in the tower building. He was sitting away from the group working on a puzzle and had just turned around and spoken. Naturally, his comment greatly intrigued me.

Before I could say anything, Angie said, "How do you know that?"

That was exactly my question, because I wasn't aware of any pattern that would just tell you that. Aaron responded, "I've been noticing that the number of rows tall depends on how many cups there are on the first row, and I counted 32 cups in that row."

Aaron demonstrated this using the cups. The children gave him full attention, because from past experience they knew he always had something important to say. "Look—one cup, one row. Two cups on the bottom and I put one on top of that, that is 2 rows tall." He then demonstrated that for three cups in the first row, the tower would be 3 rows tall, and for 4 cups on the first row, it would be 4 rows tall. He led us to see that the number of cups in the first row was always the same as the number of rows. Thus, if there were 32 cups in the first row, the tower would be 32 rows tall. As I was taking this in, Claire shifted the conversation in another direction.

"Oh," Claire said, "then there isn't going to be enough room." I thought I knew what she was thinking but I decided to pose a question.

"Why do you say that?"

"Simple," she countered. "When it was 17 rows tall, it was way up here [indicating with her outstretched hands the height of the tower]. Thirty-two rows is a lot higher." She knew a tower that was 32 rows tall would be *much* taller and thought that they wouldn't be able to build it as the classroom ceiling simply wasn't high enough.

"It might reach up there," Aaron said, "but I don't think we will have enough cups." And with this comment, Aaron shifted the focus of our investigation from the height of the tower to the number of cups needed to build it.

How Many Cups Would We Need?

"Let's figure out if we do or not," I said, referring to the number of cups needed, as I jumped in to take advantage of a teachable moment.

Aaron and Barbara thought that would be interesting to do and began to pursue it while others continued to build. They began by building a 1-row tower, a 2-row tower, and a 3-row tower of cups and counting their results. This was an interesting team: Aaron, a precocious math student, and Barbara, a great builder.

"Wait, I need my journal," Aaron cried, and he ran back to get it out of his cubby. After returning, he began to sketch out his towers and write numbers by them. He continued to sketch while Barbara built. When he finished the 4-row tower, he stopped.

"Barbara," he said, "I don't think we need to count anymore. Just imagine one more cup on each row like this." He drew it and her eyes lit up. She got it! (See Figure 9–3.)

"Yeah! This one would have 15!" Barbara said. She knew that the 4-row tower had 10 cups in all, and that putting one more cup on each row plus one on the top would add 5 more cups.

A few children stopped and watched the work, attracted by the excitement in Barbara's voice. But Aaron and Barbara continued to work. Aaron struggled to draw the picture of 5 towers. I could tell his hand was getting tired and his drawings were going to grow to the point where he no longer could draw the towers and thus would stop. I didn't want him to lose momentum, so I went over and sat down next to him. As I looked at his work, I noticed something.

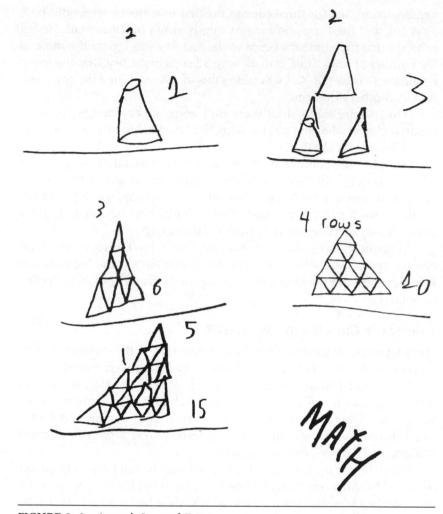

FIGURE 9–3   Aaron's Journal Entry

"Aaron," I said, "look at your work. I think I see a pattern. Look, the number of cups used in the first tower (one) plus the number of new cups used to build the next tower (two) equals the total number of cups (three). Now let's look at a 3-row tower. It will use 3 cups plus 3 new cups."

That's all I needed to say. He immediately responded, "Oh, yeah! 3 + 3 = 6, 6 + 4 = 10, 10 + 5 = 15, 15 + 6 = . . . [here he had some trouble but counted on using his fingers] "21, 21 + 7 = 28 [short pause on this one]. I got it! I don't need to draw anymore. I need a calculator!"

In my room, calculators are in a basket that is always available. Kids can just go and get one, which he did. Here I was, a teacher observing a *very* bright child figuring out a *very* big idea. Half of me was speechless and the other half was watching the clock. Only 10 minutes before dismissal time! There wouldn't be time for Aaron to complete his work today. I would have loved to see Aaron do this, so I asked him if he would be interested in finishing on Monday.

"Oh yes, but first I need to make a report," he responded. The children know they have the right to stop the class and make a report when they have something important to share. Aaron explained to the class that he and Barbara had made a discovery. (I was pleased that he included Barbara in his report.) He explained his thinking and the pattern very clearly and his plan to figure out how many cups it would take build a tower 32 rows tall.

I wondered whether any of the other children understood what he was talking about. Most of them were listening intently and a few seemed to be trying to follow his logic. However, after he finished, Kelly commented, "Then we could really just count the number of cups we have, and then we'd know how tall we really could build our tower."

Kelly's statement indicated that she had been able to take Aaron's idea and work it backward in her mind in a very practical way. She realized that if we knew the total number of cups needed we could find whether we had enough cups to build the 32-row tower.

I was pleased to see that Aaron's contributions stimulated and challenged the thinking of the rest of the children.

Aaron burst into the room on Monday and simply said, "528." That's all, just 528. But that was all he had to say. The children remembered the question, of course. His parents later told me how excited he was when he got home on Friday. He went right to his calculator and found the total.

That might have been the end of the story, but it wasn't. The children wanted to continue and find the number of cups they had. As part of their 100th-Day activities in February, they had grouped and counted their 100s collections, and the children remembered that. So, at play time, they began to count the cups, putting them in stacks of ten. Then they put groups of ten together to make hundreds until they figured out how many cups they had—311.

How High Is the Ceiling?

At this point the children's attention shifted to the height of the ceiling. Even though they didn't have enough cups, they still wanted to know if was possible to build a 32-row tower in the classroom.

Measuring the height of the room was a project in itself. Some children wanted to stack the cups to the ceiling, but I couldn't let them climb that high for safety reasons. Then they put one cup by the wall and found that a cinder block was about $1\frac{1}{2}$ cups tall. Next they counted the number of cinder blocks and added another cup for every 2 cinder blocks. That was Claire's contribution. Finally, they determined that they would not be able to build the tower.

Again, I thought the project was over. However, several days later, Masyn approached me at play time holding a small drinking cup from the bathroom sink.

"You know, Teacher, we could build that tower if we used *these* cups," he said matter-of-factly. Masyn had obviously been thinking about the problem for a while and was able to change the scale of the problem to fit the limitations of the height of the classroom. I was delighted by his approach and by the fact he had not forgotten the problem. He went over and held one against the wall and said, "I think 32 would fit." He figured that 3 of the small cups were about the same height as a cinder block. His classmates didn't pursue this because they knew Masyn was right.

Our extended investigation was finally over, but it had been a great experience for all.

LOOKING BACK | Looking Back . . .

When I reflect on this play time incident, I am reminded that Oliver Wendell Holmes said, "Man's mind stretched by a new idea never goes back to its original dimension." I really believe this to be true. From that day forward, the children discussed Aaron's conjecture that the number of cups on the bottom row determines the height of the tower every time they played with the cups.

I also viewed my class differently. I began to notice other ways they showed excellence in mathematical thinking. Aaron's work was certainly impressive. But I was equally impressed with Angie, who questioned Aaron's reasoning; Claire, who estimated; Barbara, who collaborated with Aaron and modeled his thinking; Kelly, who built on Aaron's idea; and Masyn, who found a way of building a 32-cup-high tower by changing the scale of the problem. I have come to believe that all of the students in this class were capable of operating on higher intellectual, social, and emotional levels.

This incident also changed my view of all the classes that followed this class. Each year when I mention Aaron's idea to a new class, my students show me that they are capable of doing equally robust mathematical thinking.

I recognize that two key—and often controversial—elements of my teaching made this investigation possible. The first element is my belief that the children in my class need *daily* opportunities to play. I realize that there is more and more pressure to restrict or even eliminate this traditional kindergarten activity. However, I have noticed that so many of the children's best mathematical experiences have come about either at play time or as a direct result of something that occurred at play time. Aaron's conjecture about the cups and the resulting class investigations would never have occurred if the children had not had many opportunities to freely explore the Solo® cups.

The second element is the ready availability of calculators in my kindergarten classroom. While many adults question the wisdom of allowing calculator use at such an early age, I encourage the appropriate use of calculators, not as a substitute for, but as an aid to, deeper mathematical thinking. As in this example, sometimes the most interesting mathematical investigations require repetitive or difficult computation that would impede students from seeing the underlying patterns and structure of a mathematical situation. Aaron reached a point where he was unable to compute the additional cups. Without a calculator, this investigation would have come to a frustrating end. Having a calculator readily available enabled Aaron to continue the pattern he discovered and arrive at the correct solution to a very intriguing problem. This is the real power of calculator-assisted thinking.

About the Mathematics

Aaron's mathematical insights and reasoning drove the early work forward. His first insight was the generalization that the number of cups in the bottom row of a tower is the same as the number of rows. This allowed him to conclude that the tower would be 32 rows tall. He demonstrated that the pattern was true for the first four towers. His generalization, an extension of a pattern, likely came from looking at several instances and drawing a conclusion about the general case: x cups long means the tower is x rows tall.

> Two central themes of algebraic thinking are appropriate for young students. The first involves making generalizations and using symbols to represent mathematical ideas, and the second is representing and solving problems.
>
> —*Principles and Standards for School Mathematics* (93)

His second mathematical contribution was recognizing that the number of cups required to build a tower of height x was the sum of the whole numbers from 1 to x. For a 3-row tower, one finds the sum $1 + 2 + 3$; for a 4-row tower, one finds the sum $1 + 2 + 3 + 4$. Thus, for the number of cups required to build a 32-row tower, one adds the whole numbers from 1 to 32. In developing his generalization, notice how he made use of the *building on* technique. After constructing a 3-row tower (using $1 + 2 + 3$ cups), he added 1 more cup onto each row and put one on top—a total of 4 cups. Thus, the number of cups required for a four-row tower was $1 + 2 + 3 + 4$, or 10, cups. Aaron then stated a series of number sentences in which the second addend increased by 1 each time ($3 + 3 = 6$, $6 + 4 = 10$, $10 + 5 = 15$, etc.). Even trying to explain this pattern is complex, let alone trying to understand it.

The mathematical power of Aaron's pattern is that it frees one from counting. A key thing about mathematics is that it allows us to generalize beyond the seen to the unseen—to go beyond specific cases to establish a general pattern. Although Aaron's thinking is not typical at this level, there are many young children who think in ways similar to Aaron's ways and we need to be sensitive to them.

There is one other significant aspect of the mathematics in this project, namely, finding the height of the classroom. First, for a unit of measure, the children chose something relevant to them: the height of one Solo® cup. Then they used indirect measurement. Rather than counting the number of units from floor to ceiling, which was not possible, they compared their cup unit to cinder blocks. Their thinking was based on the fact that 3 cups were as tall as two cinder blocks—that is, the ratio of cup units to cinder blocks was 3 to 2. The children dealt with this by thinking "1 cup for each cinder block and an extra cup for every 2 blocks"—a wonderful way of dealing with $1^1/_2 + 1^1/_2$. Their work reminds us that children possess intuitive knowledge of many important mathematical ideas. We need to be aware of how they think and of the content of their thinking in order to encourage and build on it.

Dear Bus Barn,

We are going to the Brookfield zoo. We need a bus with 22 benches. It must be big enough for 65 people to go to the zoo.

Thank you,
Mrs. Andrews' Class

Young students can engage in substantive problem solving and in doing so develop basic skills, higher order thinking skills, and problem solving strategies.

—*Principles and Standards for School Mathematics (103)*

10

May—"Dear Bus Barn"

Setting the Stage

It was early May and time to finalize plans for our field trip to the zoo. I had reserved the date, and now it was time to submit the bus request. I began to think of all the details—one bus or two, the size of the bus, number of chaperones, the cost per child, etc. I was *not* looking forward to dealing with these messy details.

Then my mind drifted back to a conference presentation I had attended in which the speaker talked about second graders working on a similar problem. She had reminded us that children can do far more than we give them credit for, especially when invested in a problem. In fact, they particularly enjoy really challenging problems. I knew that and I needed to act on it! I would turn the problem over to my children and let them figure it out. With that decided, I turned my attention to how I would structure the work. At the center of my thinking was having the children create a letter to the bus barn about the capacity of buses. I really liked this idea, as it would link mathematics and language arts. I was now ready to proceed.

The Problem

Open-ended lessons always involve surprises for me and the first one occurred right after I posed this problem to my morning class. As the children began to talk about the problem with one another, it was clear that they had an entirely different view of the transportation problem. Their solution was a simple one: their parents could drive them. They also had a solution to the cost of the buses: charge it! So, I realized that I had to help them understand *my* problem, namely that school policy required that students be transported by bus and that chaperones needed to ride the bus. While the initial discussion wasn't directed at solving *my* problem, I was reminded how important such preliminary discussions are in helping children settle their minds around a problem—that is, get inside of it.

How Many Children in All?

After I restated the problem, there were two quick comments:

Matt said, "Well, first we have to find out how many people will be riding the bus."

Sarah, a practical child, immediately chimed in, "Both classes, remember!"

Matt and Sarah had identified the first subproblem to be solved, and the attention of the class shifted to finding the number of children in both classes. The suggestions flew quickly and spontaneously:

"We could line up and count ourselves . . . "

"We could count the chairs . . ."

"We could count the work cups . . ."

"Counting ourselves won't work because some are absent . . ."

"Yeah [laughter] Including the whole entire P.M. class . . ."

"Counting the chairs won't work because there are just enough chairs for us . . ."

"But the afternoonies sit in the same chairs . . ."

"We could just count each one two times..."

"But there is an empty chair at our table and no kid sits in it. Maybe a kid sits there in the afternoon. Who knows!"

At this point, one child suggested counting their supply cups because their pictures and those of the afternoon students were on them. This set off sparks in Matt; he jumped up and ran to the picture graph in the front of the room.

"I got it!" he said, beaming. "Everyone is up here on this graph. We could just count here!" I had thought about suggesting this earlier but was so glad that I didn't. Again, not only did the idea come from the children, but we also had had an insightful and practical discussion that involved a variety of ideas about gathering the data.

We counted and recounted and agreed that there were 52 children. "So 52 children will go on the bus?" I asked.

"Wait," one child interjected, "we have to count the bus driver and Mrs. Andrews." So the total was adjusted to 54.

How Many Chaperones Are Needed?

"Uh-oh," said another child, "we forgot the chaperones. How many chaperones do we need?" For the next few minutes the mathematical problem was forgotten as the discussion shifted to whose mom or dad might go on the field trip, which parents had already been involved, and whether the mother of twins could go on two trips. My job was to get them back to our problem.

To recapture their attention, I said, "Now, who gets to come is a problem for another day, but the *really big* problem, the one you may not be able to figure out, is how many chaperones can go. You see, we need 1 chaperone for every 5 children, and we still want to fit them all on one bus. Do you think you could figure this out, or should I ask some fifth graders to help us?"

I had originally intended to just tell them how many chaperones we needed and have them find the new total, but I was growing more and more confident in their ability to solve difficult problems. I also thought that challenging them with a harder problem might refocus them on the math. It worked! "No! We can do it!" was the chorus. Their enthusiasm didn't surprise me, but I was surprised by what came next.

> Young children will express their conjectures and describe their thinking in their own words and often explore them using concrete materials and examples.
>
> —*Principles and Standards for School Mathematics* (57)

"We could use the counting chart!" said Kaitlyn, pointing to the large hundreds chart that was posted on the magnetic board.

I had no idea how she intended to use the chart, so I asked, "Could you tell me a bit about how we could do this?"

"No, but I can show you," Kaitlyn answered. She quickly came to the chart, grabbing a handful of magnets on her way. "We could start at 52 . . ." [She knew that teachers and bus drivers didn't need chaperones.] and count back and put a magnet on 47."[1] She placed a magnet on the chart. "That's the parent chaperone. Now count back 5 again. Here's another chaperone," she said as she put a magnet on 42. Kaitlyn continued for a couple more numbers, until Starla stopped her.

"Wait a minute! You don't need to count anymore. I see a pattern." Starla leapt up and went to the board. "See, just put a magnet here, here, here, here, . . . ," she said, pointing to 27, 22, 17, and 12 as she spoke. (See Figure 10–1.)

Some of the children were not convinced, so we had to stop and let children take turns coming to the board to check out Starla's pattern for counting back by fives. I then asked what we needed to do next. "Count

---

1   *Kaitlyn was thinking about groups of five, but in counting back five from 52, she had included both 52 and 47, thus including six numbers (52, 51, 50, 49, 48, 47). When the counting was finished, there were actually two children left over, the first person and the fifty-second person.*

Hundreds Chart

1	②	3	4	5	6	⑦	8	9	10
11	⑫	13	14	15	16	⑰	18	19	20
21	㉒	23	24	25	26	㉗	28	29	30
31	㉜	33	34	35	36	㉞	38	39	40
41	㊷	43	44	45	46	㊷	48	49	50
51	52	53	54	55	56	57	58	59	60
61	62	63	64	65	66	67	68	69	70
71	72	73	74	75	76	77	78	79	80
81	82	83	84	85	86	87	88	89	90
91	92	93	94	95	96	97	98	99	100

FIGURE 10–1   Hundreds Chart

the magnets!" the children chorused. Everyone agreed that the answer was 10, that is, 10 chaperones.

Jack said, "I disagree. What about this number?" He pointed to the 1 to the left of the last magnet. "Does this one have a chaperone?" Jack's question set off another round of comments, once again often going beyond the mathematics.

"That one can just go with the teacher."

"The teacher is not a chaperone."

"I don't think we need a chaperone for just one child."

"The rule says we have to have one chaperone for every 5 children."

"Maybe the 1 is a remainder."

"If we add another chaperone, maybe my mom could come."

"Yes, we need 11 chaperones. Add one more."

How Many People in All?

It was time for me to summarize where we were. I reminded the children that we were trying to find how many people would be going on the bus. We knew that 52 children and a teacher and a bus driver would be going—that makes 54—and we had just agreed that there would be 11 chaperones. I asked, "What do we need to do now?"

"You could just add 54 and 11 to see how many we need," Bilal suggested.

I then asked Sameer, a rather quiet child, "Sameer, do you have any ideas on how we could do that?" Sameer almost never talked. He could but simply chose not to. Talking was not his thing!

And he didn't talk today, either. He simply wiggled his ten fingers.

"We could use our fingers?" I queried.

"But we only have ten fingers, Sameer!" Sarah argued. To my great surprise, Sameer spoke.

"We could use our head for the last one," he said, nodding his head to show how to indicate the eleventh one. I wish there had been time to savor this moment, but the discussion continued.

"We could use the chart," suggested another child. "We could just put the 11 magnets on the numbers after 54 and see where the last one goes."

"We could use the number line," Starla suggested. "We could start at 54 and count 11 more numbers and that would be how many."

Well, we tried all three ways, and got the same answer each time: 65. To summarize where we were, I wrote the following on the board: "We need to take 65 people to the zoo. Will 1 bus be enough?" However, we wouldn't be able to work on this part of the problem today, as it was time to go to music class. As the children lined up to leave the room, I was already envisioning tomorrow's work: I would re-present the problem and then the children would compose a letter to the district bus administrator asking how many people could fit on one bus. But, as we shall see, the children had other ideas.

How Many People Can Fit on a Bus?

"Boys and girls," I began, "yesterday we figured out how many people are going to the zoo. Does anyone remember how many it was?" Everyone knew the answer was 65. "What do we need to do next?" I continued. I expected them to say we had to find how many people would fit on a bus, but again, I was surprised.

Bilal spoke up, "We need to figure out how many benches are on the bus."[2] This set off a delightful interchange about their experiences in riding a bus. They had only ridden a bus once before this year, as children are not bused to this school.

"I remember the last time, we sat 3 on a seat. I sat with Tony and Devin."

"Except for the last seat. That one had 2—me and my dad!"

---

2   *We used "benches" to distinguish between an individual seat and the seats that held 3 children.*

And the children were off, relating whom they sat next to on the fall trip. Bilal brought the class back to the problem when he suggested that we could use our calculators and count by 3 (using the automatic constant we had just learned about) to figure out how many benches we would need on the bus. Kevin, however, wanted to use the magnets and the counting chart again, this time putting a magnet on every third number.

We decided to do both. Bilal used the overhead calculator while Kevin put the magnets on the hundreds chart. The class watched closely to see if the numbers matched. Soon children were predicting which number would come up next, and another pattern emerged. Kevin began to place the magnets in a left diagonal pattern until he got to 63. Then he stopped. "These two [64 and 65] are the back seat," he said, referring to the bench that seated two people, and placed a magnet on 65.

After counting to find that there would need to be 22 benches on the bus, they became stuck; they had no way of knowing whether there were 22 benches on a bus. Jon commented, "I think there might be. There was a lot of them."

Finally, my moment had arrived to introduce the letter the class could send to the bus barn about the number of benches on a bus. I thought, "We will write that class letter!" I suggested to the class that we could write a letter to the bus barn and ask if there are 22 benches on a school bus. However, the letter was not to be. At that moment, Arthur spoke up.

"Why do that?" he asked, pointing to the window. "There's a school bus outside!" I couldn't believe my eyes. Because we are not a busing school, this was a rare sight. (The bus had just delivered another class after a field trip.)

"Let's go see right now!" Bilal suggested.

Well, so much for the letter; we would go in a different direction than I had planned. The class quickly lined up and we marched out to see the bus. The bus driver was leaning against it and I quickly moved toward him. I explained what we had been doing and quietly begged him *not* to tell the children what the capacity of the bus was, but to let them solve the problem for themselves. He was eager to help and even added a twist I hadn't thought of. He suggested that one child board the bus and count the seats.

"However," he said to the children, winking at me, "I am in a bit of a hurry, so I only have time for you to count the benches on only one side of the bus!" The helper of the day and the driver boarded the bus and together they counted the benches on the right side of the aisle.

As the helper exited the bus, she announced there were 11 benches on the right side. She also reported that the driver assured her that both sides of the bus had the same number of benches. After thanking the driver, back we went into the room to solve the rest of our problem.

The momentum was high! The children were clearly eager to finish solving the problem. I helped them restate the problem, and I wrote the following on the board, emphasizing the numbers and the word *same*:

We need *22* benches.
There are *11* benches on *1* side of the bus.
There is the *same number* of benches on each side.
Are there enough benches?

As the children headed back to their seats, I reminded them that they could use anything in the room to help them think about the problem. I also asked them to share their thinking with another student when they were finished. I was curious to see what strategies they would use and how they would solve the problem—particularly with no guidance from me.

There was so much to observe and "file away" for future reference. I noticed that some children worked alone and some with partners. They made use of a wide variety of approaches and materials. Some children got calculators from the basket, some got beans and cups, others went for their math journals and work cups, a few got out chalkboards, and a couple of them got the stacking circles they loved to use. The room was abuzz with the sound of thinking and talking mathematics.

Their processes and strategies were also fascinating. Some children drew an interior map of the bus, showing two sides with 11 benches on each side, and wrote "22." One child drew a picture of a bus with lots of children inside, but I didn't see any evidence of her attempt to solve the problem. I said, "My! That's a lot of children. About how many will you draw?"

"I think I will draw 11 and then 11 more," she said. And she did! She apparently used 1 child to represent 3 children.

Two children worked with the stacking circles. Each stacked 11 circles then measured the stack against each other's. When the stacks appeared even, they took turns counting all the pieces and were delighted when the count was 22. "Whew!" they said. "Just enough!" And off they went to record their work in their math journals.

Some used only symbols. One child entered "11 + 11 =" in his calculator and got "22." He showed several people how to do this. A couple of children wrote

$$\begin{array}{r} 11 \\ + 11 \\ \hline 22 \end{array}$$

Some children made 2 groups of 11 tally marks on their chalkboards and counted them.

卌 卌 /
卌 卌 /

Two children used the hundreds chart. They first counted out 11 magnets each and then took turns putting these magnets on the chart, starting at 1. "Look! We barely just have enough!" they exclaimed.

The whole process of finding the sum was a wonderful assessment opportunity. I was particularly interested in the ways the children used the cubes. Three children used connecting cubes but in somewhat different ways. The first child counted out a pile of 11 cubes and stacked them up. She then made another stack, without counting, and measured it against the first stack until the two were even. Finally, she counted both stacks, starting at one. Another child counted out 2 piles of 11 cubes, stacked them both up, measured to be sure they were even, and then counted on from the first stack (11—12, 13, 14, . . . 21, 22). The third child made one stack of 11 red cubes, counting and recounting to make sure he had 11. Then he made another stack of white cubes as tall as the first stack. Then he disassembled the cubes and restacked them in an AB pattern, and finally counted them, starting at 1. I often see children do this and asked a child once why he did it. He explained to me that making a pattern of alternating colors made it easier for him to count. Perhaps the cubes stand out better and the child can tell which ones he has counted.

The next day the children shared their strategies for solving the problem and all came to an agreement that we would indeed all fit onto one bus. And guess what? We finally *did* write that letter, requesting a bus with 22 benches that would carry 65 people to the zoo!

Our three days of solving the bus problem were at an end. Time did not permit the children to help me figure out how much each child would have to pay, but I have no doubt that they could have!

LOOKING BACK

Looking Back . . .

I am continually surprised by what my children do with the tasks I present. I guess this is why I find teaching so exciting. I had a plan for this lesson, but I also wanted the children to take ownership of the task—to investigate the problem in ways that made sense to them. However, as this experience points out, one of the consequences of letting children take ownership is that they often go in unexpected directions! Real investigations do not always move in a straight line, nor do they always follow a prescribed path. At these times I have to let go of my plans and allow the children to take side trips and detours. Letting go doesn't mean *standing back*, however.

Throughout these three days, there were several times when I had to make quick decisions to change directions, select particular ideas to emphasize or highlight, and manage the direction of the work, while at the same time being careful to leave it in the hands of the children. This is hard work. Sometimes it feels like I am aiming at a moving target! And it's also time-consuming. The lesson I had envisioned as taking one day stretched out over three days. It might have been more efficient to move the class along quickly. However, I think that allowing them the time to look at this problem from different angles—play with it, talk about it, and work on it together—and choose the tools they were comfortable using really paid off in the end. I have come to think that time spent in thought is never wasted.

About the Mathematics

This problem-solving experience, which arose in the context of a classroom situation, is an excellent example of the amount of mathematics that can be involved in the solution of such problems—determining the number of children in two classes; the number of chaperones; the total number of bus riders; the number of benches on the bus; and the number of people the bus would hold. To do this, children used number sense, dealt with fundamental ideas of operations, worked with ratios (1 chaperone for every 5 children) and remainders, and added two-digit numbers.

There is a perception by some that work with numbers, operations, and computation *must* occur in structured, focused lessons in order to be productive. We are reminded that children possess wonderful insights and informal mathematical concepts gained through their everyday and in-school applied experiences. Further, their informal mathematical ideas can be strengthened through such opportunities.

One must be impressed by the inventiveness and purposefulness of children's problem solving, particularly when they care about the problem they are solving. The richness of their mathematical reasoning and the variety of the strategies they used is also impressive. They used a variety of tools (counters, stacking cubes, hundreds charts, tally marks, and symbols) to support their reasoning and employed a variety of counting and computational strategies.

We can only wonder what would have happened if there had been time for them to find how much each child would have had to pay.

[Children] . . . should continue to explore the capacity of various containers by direct comparisons or by counting the number of scoops or cups required to fill each one. They also should experiment with filling larger containers with the contents of smaller ones and conjecture whether a quantity may be too much for a proposed container.

—Principles and Standards
for School Mathematics (104)

11

June—Revisiting the Rice Table

Setting the Stage

The school year was winding down; only one week left of kindergarten. It was time to start closing up some of the centers to prepare the room for summer cleaning. Instead of doing this work all by myself, I like to include the children in the work. This cleanup time offers opportunities to revisit the experiences we had at each center.

It was now time to close down the rice table and a good opportunity to learn what the students had gained from their work at this center throughout the year. I thought back to our initial experience in the fall. I had introduced a lot of big ideas about measurement—the notion of a unit, the measurement process, comparing containers to see which held more or less, and so on. I also remember one child's comment about capacity being related to whether the material was solid or liquid. That comment had led me to alternate rice and water as materials at this table. I wondered how many children still held to this belief.

Today was a good time to have the children share some of their memories about the work and to have a culminating activity that would call forth all the children had learned this year at the rice table.

The Lesson

Sharing Memories

"Which center is closing today?" Dane asked. He knew that each time we had gathered in a circle this week, we had reminisced about a different center before closing it up. So far, we had closed the listening center, the housekeeping center, and the science center.

"Well, I'm sad to say it's the rice table," I answered.

I was used to the children's groans. None of the children seemed to want their kindergarten experience to end.

"Who would like to tell a story about the rice table?" I asked.

Many hands went up.

"I liked filling up all the bottles with water," Masyn said. "I liked the water best."

I laughed as I recalled how hard it was to keep Masyn from splashing in the water at first and how I had almost closed down the water before it was even open. He soon learned it was fun to fill those containers, and he tried to fill all 20 each time he visited this center.

"I liked it when we colored the rice," said Rebecca, referring to the time in the winter when I had replaced the water with rice again. The children were not happy about this change, so I decided that coloring the rice might spice things up. We dyed one tubful of the rice red. It seemed to do the trick. "I made an AB pattern in my bottle—red-white-red-white," Rebecca continued.

"Oh, estimitating the rice!" Delon said. "I just love estimitating!" (And I loved his way of saying "estimating.")

Delon went on to describe an activity in which the children chose a jar or a bottle and predicted the level of the rice if 5 scoops of rice were put inside. They would mark their estimate with a sticky dot or a piece of tape and then test their prediction. Knowing they were free to move the dot to adjust their initial prediction as they added scoops freed them of the fear of being wrong.

"I liked counting the scoops best," Elizabeth offered. The children's nods indicated they were remembering the activity in which they were challenged to measure how many scoops some containers held and then record this amount on a paper on which outlines of those containers had been drawn.

As Elizabeth talked, I remembered the day when one child brought me his completed record sheet. I was puzzled by the marks next to the picture of a bottle and questioned him about it. (See Figure 11–1.)

"Oh, that jar held $10^1/_2$ scoops, Teacher." His symbol for $10^1/_2$ was certainly not the standard representation, but it was effective at communicating his idea.

FIGURE 11–1   Child's Representation of $10^1/_2$

The children continued to describe experiences at the rice table. Leslie remembered when it was her turn to take a container home to find something at her house that held a little more or a little less than the jar she had chosen. "My toy canteen held a little more than jar B."

Oh, I had forgotten that one! At first, I recalled, the children tended to bring in objects that held *a lot* more or less. Soon, however, the children brought in items that held just *a little* more or less.

"Remember Aaron's Turn Over game?" Sarah asked.

Everybody laughed as we recalled the day Aaron brought in a half-empty syrup bottle. He had put a small sticky dot at the "fill line." He had then asked me where I thought the fill line would be if he turned the bottle upside down! Predicting and then watching the syrup flow into place had been fascinating, and the children repeated this game at the rice table for days.

"Oh, my gosh!" I thought, looking at the clock. We had become involved in our recollections, but I needed to save time for the final activity that I had planned. The children had been sitting for a while, but I thought they would still be able to concentrate on the activity.

Ordering Containers

I led the children in some stretching exercises and then had them sit down in a new place in the circle. While the children found a place in the circle, I placed 8 paper plates in a straight row in the middle of the circle. Then I placed 7 containers from the rice table randomly on the plates, leaving one empty plate at the end of the row. (See Figure 11–2.)

I said, "Now, before I put these containers away, boys and girls, I want to put them in order by how much they hold. I know I could go to the rice table and measure to find out, but I would like to see if you could help me figure this out without putting any rice into the containers."

I explained further, "Our job is to move the containers around so that they are in order of capacity—that is, by how much they hold. I would like the container that holds the most to be here." I motioned to the first plate to my left in the line.

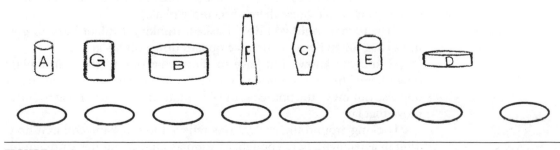

FIGURE 11–2

"Then the one that holds the next most goes here?" asked Jenny, pointing to the plate to the right of the one I had indicated.

"Exactly! Each jar that holds a little less will go on the next plate, until the jar that holds the least is last," I explained.

"That's cinchy!" Claire said. "Can I do it?"

"That *would* be cinchy," I agreed, "if only one person got to do the job and could move as many jars and bottles as you wanted. But that wouldn't be fair and that wouldn't be very challenging."

I continued, "In my game, each of you will have a turn, *but*—and here comes the challenge—you may move only *one* jar when it is your turn. Everybody will have to cooperate to get these containers in the correct order. We will keep going around the circle until we all agree. We may need to go around more than once for this to happen. When it is your turn, you may move any one jar you think you need to. If it is not your turn, you may not touch any of the jars. If you think the jars are in the correct order, then you may pass."

"Wait! What goes on the extra plate?" Kelly asked. "There are only 7 jars and 8 plates!"

"That's a very good question, Kelly," I said. "Can anyone figure out why we might need that extra plate?"

The class was quiet for a minute, and their silence made me nervous.

Had I made this task too difficult? Perhaps I should have let them move two jars at a time. Putting them in order would certainly be simple if they could do this.

I was about ready to change my rule when Starla spoke up.

"I know. Like if I wanted to move a jar from where it is and I can only move one, I have to have a place to move it!"

That made sense to the rest of the class, but I could tell from their expressions that they didn't quite see how this game was going to work. "Oh, well," I thought, "nothing ventured, nothing gained!" After clarifying the rules and the goals again, we were ready to start, with the helper of the day having the first turn. Lindsay hesitated for a long while, then picked up the third jar in line and held it in her hand.

"I want to put this one first cause it holds the most," she said, frustrated. "But I can't 'cause there's no empty plate."

"Then what could you do?" I asked, thinking I might need to give her a clue. Julian began to bounce up and down on his knees.

"I know! I know! You have to move that one to the empty plate down here!" he said, pointing to the last plate in the row. "Then someone else can move the bottle on the first plate, then there will be room to move that jar!"

Looking around the circle, I was relieved to see some children nodding in agreement. Sure enough, as soon as Lindsay sat her jar down on the last plate, the next person in the circle moved the first jar in line to the empty plate, and the next person moved Lindsay's jar from the last plate to the first. It looked like they might be catching on to how this activity worked, and I began to relax—but not for long. On the next move, Brett moved Lindsay's jar back to the last plate, and on the next turn, Elizabeth moved the fourth container, which was tall and thin, to the front of the line.

"Oh no!" I thought. "They've worked all year with these containers and they still think the tallest bottle holds the most." (I had carefully selected 7 bottles and jars of different heights, widths, and variations; this one was a tall, thin bottle that had held bubble bath.) It was obvious to me that this bottle would not hold the most, but not to this child. I wondered if other children would immediately disagree. Part of me hoped so.

They didn't. The next child concentrated on moving a small bottle to the empty plate. Several other moves were made before it was Kelly's turn. She went right for that bubble bath bottle and moved it from its first-place position. The next child moved Lindsay's jar from the last plate to the now-empty first plate.

"Oh good!" I thought silently. "Now we are getting somewhere."

But Nabihah was next, and she took that jar right back off!

Next came Delon, who used his turn to move the tall bottle right back to the first plate! This was turning into a battle of the wills as each child in turn silently maneuvered these two containers back and forth off the first plate. This activity was accompanied by laughter, and for a minute I was afraid that the focus had become to continue the joke of moving the tall bottle back and forth. I was soon to be proven wrong, when Prateek reversed Claire's move in which she had taken the tall bottle from first place and put it on the empty middle plate.

"No!" Claire said. "Don't let him move mine. I had it right!" she said to me, pleadingly. I could tell by her tone that she was really getting frustrated.

"Claire," I said, "if you disagree with what Prateek did, I would like you to tell him, not me. I will be interested to hear what you have to say."

I hoped this remark would give Claire a minute to calm down and help the class refocus on the goal. I didn't want to be the referee in this game; I wanted the children to talk with one another about the problem. But I also wanted to let Claire know that I cared about her ideas and would be listening.

This comment seemed to turn the tide. Instead of just moving the containers, Claire (and the other children) began focusing on the reasons for their moves.

"See," Claire explained, as calmly as she could, "that tall bottle is skinny at the top so it won't hold much rice up there."

"But look at that jar," she said, pointing to the one she thought held more. "It's wide across the bottom and it's that way all the way to the top. I think it will hold the most because it is widest."

"But," said Prateek, defending his move, "I remember filling that jar and it only held 6 cups of rice. Sammy was my partner and she had a tall bottle that held more scoops than mine did."

"That couldn't be possible," I thought to myself. Perhaps Prateek was confused or just saying that in defense of his choice. Then it occurred to me that he could be right. It was my turn to ask a question of Prateek.

"Do you remember which measuring cup you used?"

"That's it!" Sammy said, beaming. "I used the orange one and you used the tan one, Prateek. Remember?"

"Why would that matter?" I couldn't resist asking.

"Well," Prateek answered, "the tan scoop was larger." He hesitated a few moments while the children patiently waited.

Then he moved the tall bottle back to the first plate. On Sarah's turn, she left it where it was and concentrated on placing another container in order.

This activity went back and forth like this for a very long time, much longer than I had anticipated. (I was glad that my schedule was a bit looser on this last week of school.) The children began to talk with one another, planning their moves ahead of time. They had realized that it took two turns to accomplish a move and were beginning to collaborate on how to get the jars in the order they thought was correct. There was intense discussion about the capacity of the jars. When it was Aaron's turn, he turned his container over. "I'm trying to imagine where the rice would come to if the bottles are upside down," he explained.

> By allowing time for thinking, believing that young students can solve problems, listening carefully to their explanations, and structuring an environment that values the work that students do, teachers promote problem solving and help students make their strategies explicit.
>
> —*Principles and Standards for School Mathematics* (119)

I had to smile to myself at the memory of his Turn Over game. Here he was using this technique to help him consider the placement of the last few containers, all of which were pretty similar in height, but not in shape.

"OK, guys," he announced. "I think this one goes second, but I can't put it there yet."

He then moved the container on the second plate down to the empty plate. Immediately the next child moved Aaron's jar to the second place.

The children continued to take turns, giving reasons for their moves. If a child forgot, another child would usually ask. Occasionally a child would pass, indicating that in his or her opinion, the containers were in the right order. We made several more trips around the circle, until finally everyone was satisfied that the jars were in order of capacity.

"Well, we are all agreed then," I said, starting to pick up the containers.

Checking the Solution

"Wait!" Cameron said. "We've got to find out!" The rest of the children agreed. They were incredulous that I would think of putting the jars and bottles away before we checked to see if their answer was correct. I had hoped this would happen and I was prepared for it.

"OK, I guess we have to prove it. How could we do that?" I inquired innocently.

Elizabeth thought we should count how many scoops went into each bottle and make a chart. "Then we can see which number is highest, then next highest," she explained.

Masyn spoke up. "Just take two." Here was the child who had spent the better part of the year filling up all the jars, and now he wanted to fill only two. However, when I asked him to explain this method, he seemed unable to do so.

"Do you mean we could fill two containers with rice and see which one holds more scoops?" I asked, trying to be helpful.

A negative nod told me I was wrong.

"I think I know what you mean, Masyn," Jenny said. "Do you mean we could compare like we did when we brought something from home?"

Sarah's question was rewarded with a smile from Masyn, who then added, "Yeah, like fill the one that holds most, then pour it into the other one."

Masyn had hit on my plan. I had intended to suggest, as a challenge to the children, that they try to figure out a way to determine the order of capacity by filling only one container.

Since Masyn had the idea, he got to choose one container to fill. I held my breath as I saw him waver between the wide jar that now occupied first place and that dratted tall bottle. He finally picked up the jar and filled it to the top—21 scoops and a little bit more. Then he poured this rice into the next container. When it was completely filled, all could see that some rice remained in the first jar.

"So what does that prove?" I asked the class. They were eager to tell me that the jar held more than the second container.

"Or else," Kirsten explained, "there wouldn't be any left in the bottle." Nods all around convinced me that most understood this proof.

Kirsten did the honors of checking the second bottle with the third, and so it went. Each time there was a little rice left in the "control" bottle— that is, until we got the fifth bottle.

"Hey! This one held all the rice and there's even more room!" Jeff reported.

"So what does that mean?" I asked him. Jeff didn't seem to know, so I asked if anybody could help Jeff understand what had happened.

Several children could explain, and Jeff swapped the fourth and fifth containers and we moved on. With only one exception, the children had put those containers in descending order of capacity and they were proud of their accomplishment. We just sat there a moment and looked at our work. Glancing at the clock, I knew I wouldn't have time to follow up on this last question, but I couldn't resist asking it.

"I wonder what would have happened if we had used water instead of rice."

I looked over at Sarah to see her reaction. This child, who in the fall believed a jar would hold more depending on whether its contents were liquid or solid, laughed. "Oh, I tried that, Teacher. It won't make any difference. The jar will still hold the most."

"Can we try it?" Masyn asked eagerly.

Well, we couldn't because time had caught up with us again. The children sighed and helped me pick up the plates, jars, and bottles and store them all inside the rice table. Another bittersweet sigh was heard when I dumped the rice into the trash can. (I think it was my own!)

"You know," Kelly said as she gave me her regular hug on her way out the door, "I think we could have started with the smallest jar, too."

LOOKING BACK

Looking Back . . .

The children were so proud of themselves for completing this challenge, but not nearly as proud as I was! At first I questioned my own plan, thinking it was too difficult. I am glad that I didn't underestimate the children. The complexity of the task appealed to their growing love of "hard fun." An initially difficult aspect of the problem was the level of cooperation required to solve the problem. It would have been so much simpler—and less time-consuming—to let the children swap two containers. The restriction of moving only one complicated matters greatly and necessitated communication and collaboration with the person who had the next turn. I even observed groups of 4 and 5 children talking together to plan future moves. If these children had not been used to talking and listening to one another, this task would have been impossible.

I was also thrilled to see how much they had remembered about the capacity of the jars and how well they were able to explain their reasoning about this. Their work confirmed to me again that the many hours they had spent at the rice table had really paid off. If they had not had these multiple experiences over time (some free, some informal, and some structured), there is no way they could have accomplished this task. The rice/water table experience is, on the surface, a simple one: children filling containers with rice or water. However, I believe it is my job to get the children to think deeply about simple things, not shallowly about a lot of things. They certainly showed me on this day how deeply they had been thinking about all the mathematics I had woven into this simple activity. It was really thrilling to see how far they had come this year. These children had truly become a community of learners.

> Students respond to the challenge of high expectations, and mathematics should be taught for understanding rather than around preconceptions about children's limitations.
>
> —*Principles and Standards for School Mathematics* (77)

About the Mathematics

The children certainly grew during the year in their understanding of the measurement process with respect to capacity. They were fluent with the ideas of unit, comparing the unit to the object, and reporting the number of units. In the story Piatcek thought one container held less than another because he found it held 6 scoops while Sammy's jar held more than 6 scoops. Sammy pointed out that they had used different-size scoops (or units) and there was the sense that when using a larger unit, the jar would hold a smaller number of scoops. The relationship between the size of the unit and the number of units contained in an object is an important idea that many children have difficulty with later in their school experience when converting from one unit to another.

The lesson focused on comparing and ordering containers with respect to capacity. These experiences are important in developing an understanding of an attribute and the measurement process. The ordering task was a complex one that involved transitivity. When children reasoned that if A holds more than B and B holds more than C, then A must hold more than C, they were using the transitive principle. This relationship can be symbolized as follows: If A > B and B > C, then A > C.

It was also powerful to see, from a mathematical perspective, the way the children persevered with a complex task, rather than seeking help or giving up. The willingness to press on when dealing with complex tasks is important at all levels of mathematics. Perhaps their belief that mathematics makes sense, which had been growing for ten months, was a factor in persevering with challenging tasks and even enjoying tasks that were challenging, but attainable. It was "hard fun."

References

Andrews, Angela. 1999. "Solving Geometric Problems by Using Unit Blocks." *Teaching Children Mathematics* 5(February): 318–23.

Hutchins, Pat. 1986. *The Doorbell Rang.* New York: Greenwillow Books.

McGovern, Ann. 1986. *Stone Soup.* Illustrated by Winslow Pels. New York: Scholastic.

National Council of Teachers of Mathematics. 2000. *Principles and Standards for School Mathematics.* Reston, VA: National Council of Teachers of Mathematics.

Papert, Seymour. 1996. *The Connected Family: Bridging the Digital Generation Gap.* Atlanta: Longstreet.